CULTURES OF THE WORLD

IRAN

Vijeya Rajendra and Gisela Kaplan

MARSHALL CAVENDISH
New York • London • Sydney

Reference edition published 1994 by
Marshall Cavendish Corporation
2415 Jerusalem Avenue
P.O. Box 587
North Bellmore
New York 11710

© Times Editions Pte Ltd 1993

Originated and designed by
Times Books International, an imprint of
Times Editions Pte Ltd

Printed in Singapore

Library of Congress Cataloging-in-Publication Data:
Rajendra, Vijeya, 1936–
    Iran / Vijeya Rajendra and Gisela Kaplan.
      p. cm.—(Cultures Of The World)
    Includes bibliographical references and index.
    Summary: Explores the geography, history,
government, economy, people, and culture of Iran.
      ISBN 1-85435-534-1 (vol.): —ISBN 1-85435-529-5 (set)
      1. Iran—Juvenile literature. [1. Iran.]
I. Kaplan, Gisela. II. Title. III. Series.
DS254.5.R35 1992
955—dc20   92–10207
                CIP
                AC

Cultures of the World

Editorial Director	Shirley Hew
Managing Editor	Shova Loh
Editors	Tan Kok Eng
	Leonard Lau
	Siow Peng Han
	Sue Sismondo
	MaryLee Knowlton
Picture Editor	Yee May Kaung
Production	Edmund Lam
Design	Tuck Loong
	Ang Siew Lian
	Ong Su Ping
Illustrators	Suzana Fong
	Kelvin Sim
MCC Editorial Director	Evelyn M. Fazio

INTRODUCTION

IRAN IS THE MODERN NAME of the magical world of Persia. Situated high among the mountains and plateaus in the Middle East, it is one of the world's oldest countries with a history dating back to biblical times. In ancient times, Persian kings ruled over a huge empire which included most of southwest Asia, parts of Africa and Europe.

Arab conquest of Iran introduced Islam, with Iranians becoming devout Moslems and making the religion a part of their life. However, they showed their independent spirit by following their own version of Islam (Shiism) and retaining their own language called Farsi. The discovery of oil in the early decades of the 20th century brought not only new-found wealth for the Iranians, but also embroiled Iran in European politics and intrigues.

The Shah tried to modernize his country, but religious leaders, unhappy with the way Iran was progressing, gathered enough support among the people to bring about a revolution in 1979. This resulted in the founding of the Islamic Republic of Iran, ruled mainly by a class of religious leaders.

As part of the series *Cultures of the World*, this book is an introduction to Iran and its people, their lifestyle, language and customs.

● Tehran

CONTENTS

When Iran was Persia, its kings ruled over much of the Middle East and parts of Africa, Europe and Central Asia. This bas-relief in Persepolis shows ambassadors from Syria and Lydia paying tribute to the Persian king, Darius the Great.

CONTENTS

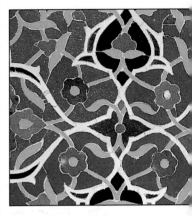

Decorations in a mosque. Islam renewed a fading Persian culture by bringing Arab patronage to Persian art, riches from distant lands and new knowledge from scientific discoveries.

GEOGRAPHY

IRAN IS IN SOUTHWEST ASIA bounded by Iraq and Turkey to the west and Afghanistan and Pakistan to the east. The Soviet Union and the Caspian Sea are to the north while the Persian Gulf and the Gulf of Oman lie in the south. It is the 16th largest country in the world and is more than twice the size of Texas.

Unlike most oil producing states of the Middle East, Iran has a substantial population of around 52 million people scattered over 636,296 square miles. Much of the land is desert.

Iran's strategic position between Asia and the lands of Europe and the Mediterranean attracted the interest of great powers like Great Britain and Russia at a time when empire building was at its peak.

For hundreds of years, the overland trade routes crossed northern Iran exposing it to the cultures of many countries. However, the frontiers of Iran gradually were eroded during the 19th century by its powerful neighbors. Iran today is only a shadow of the great country it used to be.

Opposite: **A fisherman's family by the Caspian Sea. The Caspian is not really a sea, but the largest lake in the world. Its salty waters are rich in tuna and sturgeon fish.**

Left: **Some nomads in Iraq still lead a roaming existence, traveling from place to place to find new pastures and markets for their produce. The cloudless blue skies and rocky terrain are typical of the Iranian landscape.**

The city of Tehran lies by the slopes of the majestic Elburz Mountains.

AN ANCIENT LAND

Lofty peaks and jagged mountains together with barren deserts and volcanic cones create a strange landscape. The main volcanic peak is Mount Damavand, the highest mountain in Iran, which is covered with snow throughout the year. So awesome looking is Mount Damavand, that ancient Iranians told tales of demons and heroes that lived on the mountain. Other volcanoes include Sahand and lesser Ararat, both of which show some traces of activity. Iran also lies in a major earthquake zone and, from time to time, the country is convulsed by devastating tremors. In 1990, one of the world's worst earthquakes struck north-western Iran, killing around 40,000 people.

This ancient land has long held valuable resources. The most important resource is petroleum. Long ago, when escaping gas from oil flows was set alight by lightning, it so amazed early Iranians that they began to worship fire. Early Iranian temples had an eternal flame which was used as part of their worship.

The country's most important mineral

is copper which is mined at Isfahan, Tarum and Hamadan. It is estimated that Iran has 800 million tons of good quality copper. Other minerals include chromite, iron, manganese, gold, tin, tungsten, asbestos and alumina. Important quantities of phosphates and sulphur have also been discovered. Iran's deserts have plentiful supplies of salt.

MOUNTAINS AND DISAPPEARING RIVERS

The Iranian plateau dominates most of the country. It rises about 1,500 feet above sea level. Mountain ranges encircle nearly all sides of the plateau. To the north is the Elburz Range with Iran's highest peak, Mount Damavand, rising to 18,386 feet (5605 meters). Iran's largest mountain range, the Zagros, lies west of the plateau. It is also Iran's longest range. In the past, these mountains formed natural barriers which protected the country from invasions.

Iran's only navigable river is the Karun which has its source in the Zagros Mountains. It empties into the Persian Gulf. Part of the Karun flows into the Shatt al-Arab, a tributary which forms part of the border between Iran and Iraq. This waterway has been the cause of many disputes between the two countries.

There are four main drainage basins in Iran. They are the Caspian Sea, the Persian Gulf, Lake Urmiyeh and the great desert basins. However, most of the rivers do not actually empty into any of these large bodies of water, but drain toward the plateau where they form salt lakes and salt deserts.

In contrast to the more arid regions of Iran, sparkling rivers flow through lush forests and green meadows on the Elburz Range. The high slopes catch the rain from clouds that blow in from the Caspian Sea.

The Farah Dam helps to provide water for irrigation and electricity. Dams are essential as water is scarce and many rivers dry up in the summer heat. Many people still have to rely on the old-fashioned but reliable *qanats* or underground tunnels that "pipe" water to villages and farmlands.

These salt lakes are called *namaks* and *kavirs*. *Namaks* are often shallow salt lakes, but the *kavirs* are muddy salt lakes which are treacherous because of their sticky slime. The salt that rises from these lakes shines brightly in the harsh Iranian sun often blinding visitors to the area. In fact, one of these *kavirs* called the Kavir-e-Bozorg, or the Great Kavir, gave rise to the story of Lot. According to legend, the city of Lot (also known as Sodom in the Bible) was buried under a mountain of salt as a result of a terrible curse from God who was angered by the sinful behavior of the people.

Freshwater lakes are exceedingly rare in Iran. Water is vital in this harsh land, and in order to preserve it, early Iranians developed a clever system of irrigation using qanats ("kah-NUTS"). These are long underground tunnels which carry water used to cultivate the land. *Qanats* were also built to drain some of the water from the foot of the mountains to fields and villages.

In recent years, as part of Iran's modernization program, the government has constructed a number of great dams which not only provide water for irrigation, but also are used to supply water and electricity for many new cities which have sprung up in recent times.

CLIMATE

Iran, which lies within subtropical latitudes, is a land of extremes. This is because of Iran's location in the vast Asian landmass and the effect of encircling mountain ranges which shut out any moderating oceanic influences. Rainfall is restricted to the winter months, from November to early April, and rains are limited to light showers. The Iranian plateau

receives only about 12 inches or less of rain a year. The desert areas which cover most of Iran receive less than five inches of rain a year. Most places experience hot summers and cold winters.

Much of the rain falls in areas to the north of Iran, near the Caspian Sea, and to the west. The remainder of the country gets little rain. Many people in the valleys depend on water from melting snow in the mountains for agricultural and personal use.

Tehran and Isfahan have a mean January temperature of about 68 F, but days can get very hot and night temperatures can plunge. Frost is common during the months of November to March, with snow in the mountains for most of the year. The skies over Iran are usually clear and cloudless for lack of moisture.

The Caspian Sea coast is the only area which has sufficient rainfall to support crops without irrigation. Here the climate is relatively mild. It is also the cloudiest and foggiest region of Iran.

The Iranians dread the cold because keeping warm is becoming very expensive. Most houses are not heated; their occupants keep warm by using a pan or brazier containing slow-burning coal.

Trees grow in abundance by the Caspian Sea. Only in this region are the houses traditionally made from wood and not mud.

IRAN'S FLORA AND FAUNA

Iran's vegetation reflects the country's geography, climate and position between Asia and Africa. As 75% of Iran is either arid or semi-arid, shrubs and thorn plants are common. Some of these shrubs produce useful everyday substances. Among these are licorice, gum and camel's thorn which yields manna. Poppy, sesame and absinthe are often used for flavor when cooking, while henna, saffron and indigo are traditional coloring agents.

Many of the shrubs of Iran are either spiny or prickly to prevent loss of moisture. In the salt regions, plants are resistant to both salt and drought. One useful plant is the tamarind which is used as a souring agent in cooking. At higher elevations fields of grass as well as a wide range of herbs thrive.

The rose is the most popular flower of Iran, and it is beautifully represented in miniature paintings and carpets. It grows wild as do orchids, irises, buttercups, crocuses, geraniums and gladioli.

In the forest of the Caspian area there are oak, elm, fig, walnut, maple, wild pear and plum trees. Pistachio trees grow very well here, and the export of pistachio nuts has become an important industry.

From a distance, the forests look bare, but many of the slopes have an amazing variety of native plants. Unfortunately, like many areas of the world, the forests have been cleared and used for the manufacture of paper and fuel as well as for the construction of buildings. The Iranian government has embarked on an extensive reforestation program including the planting of bushes and fodder plants.

Iran is the home of many wild animals. The southern Zagros Mountains were the home of the lion which, unfortunately, has become extinct in Iran mainly due to the sport of hunting supported by former kings and wealthy Iranians. Tigers live in the sub-tropical forests of the Caspian area, but as

forests are being cleared, the tiger too is in danger of becoming extinct. Panthers still roam many areas of Iran, but the population of cheetahs and leopards is dwindling. Jackals, hyenas, wolves and bears have managed to survive human's encroachment into their natural habitat. Other native animals include the antelope, ibex, wild ass, wild pig and wild goat.

Otters swim the rivers of the Zagros Mountains while trout gather in abundance in the mountain streams. Apart from the famous sturgeon, there are also large supplies of white fish, herring and salmon.

Many varieties of birds can be found in Iran such as the sparrow, nightingale, shrike, eagle, vulture, owl, partridge, pelican and singing birds called *bulbuls*.

Pastures lying in the shadow of mountain ranges are ideal for rearing sheep. The dry and less fertile deserts of the interior are more suitable for the hardy goats, camels and donkeys.

HISTORY

IN 1971, THE SHAH OF IRAN invited all heads of state and distinguished guests to help celebrate the 2,500th anniversary of the Persian monarchy. Never had the guests been treated to such a spectacular display of pageantry and feasting. They saw the ruins of Persepolis, the great capital of ancient Persia, and marveled at the architectural achievement of one of Iran's most famous kings, Shah Abbas, at Isfahan. They mingled with royalty, viewing the magnificent gardens for which Iran was famous and admiring Persian carpets that used colors so delicately and effectively. They listened to poetry recitals and heard stories of Iran's glorious past.

The Shah, Mohammed Reza Pahlavi, must have been filled with pride showing off his country. He was known to his people as *Shahan-Shah*— King of Kings. Yet, less than 10 years later, this monarchy came to an ignoble end with the Shah forced to flee his country. He died in exile a few years later.

Opposite: **The Gate of All Nations at Persepolis, the capital of the Achaemenid Empire that stretched from Libya and Egypt in Africa to Thrace and Macedonia in the Mediterranean and spanned the ancient trade routes in Central Asia.**

Below: **Life in the court of Darius the Great.**

LAND OF THE ARYANS

It began about 2,000 years before the birth of Christ with the coming of the Aryans. They were large bands of tribesmen who migrated from the southern steppes of Russia to settle in the area we call Iran today. The name Iran comes from the ancient Persian *Aryânâm* which means "the lands of the Aryans." The Aryan nomads gave rise to two separate groups—the Medes who settled in the north and the east, and the Persians who occupied the area to the south.

The Persians, led by Cyrus the Great, rebelled against the powerful Medes and Cyrus made himself master of the country. He founded a new dynasty called the Achaemenid ("AH-KAY-me-nid") dynasty and the conquered Medes also became known as Persians.

The Persians learned from the cultures of the civilizations they conquered, bringing cedar from Lebanon, ivory from Africa and artisans from Babylon and Greece. This sculpture reminds us of the glory that was Persepolis.

THE ACHAEMENID EMPIRE

By 539 B.C., Cyrus had conquered vast areas of land including Babylonia, Palestine, Syria and Asia Minor. In the Bible, Cyrus was mentioned as the liberator of Jews who had been held captive in Babylon. He was also noted for his humane policies, one of which allowed his conquered subjects to keep their own religion. In fact, the Persians learned and adopted much from the arts and architecture of these distant lands and enriched Persian culture. In peacetime, the Persians built magnificent buildings, excellent roads for good communications and even established shipping lines.

Darius the Great and Xerxes ("ZERK-ses") were other well-known Persian kings who expanded the empire even further so that it became the

The tomb of Darius the Great. A powerful personality and a dynamic ruler, Darius was the first Persian ruler to cross from Asia Minor to invade Europe.

largest empire of the time. Persian soldiers were much admired for their bravery. They were skillful archers. In war, ranks of bowmen would shoot hundreds of arrows at the enemy from a long distance, thus overwhelming them before the hand-to-hand fighting began. The Persians though, were unable to defeat the Greek city states and were driven back twice by the numerically inferior Greeks at Marathon and Salamis.

This great empire came to an end with the conquest of the Persians by Alexander the Great. He was only 20 years old when he himself became king. He set out to conquer the world with great enthusiasm and won nearly all his battles. Alexander's conquest of Persia was easy as it was in a state of decline. But he admired the Persians so much he married a Persian princess named Roxana and encouraged many of his generals to marry the daughters of Persian nobles.

Alexander died in 323 B.C. at the age of 32. He left no heir. His generals fought among themselves to gain control of his vast empire. Finally, one of his generals called Seleucus triumphed and founded the Seleucid dynasty.

Alexander the Great was a warrior of legendary qualities. At the age of 20, he set out from the small state of Macedonia to conquer the largest empire in the ancient world.

SELEUCIDS AND PARTHIANS

Unlike Alexander, the Seleucids were not popular. There were constant rebellions against their rule, especially from the wandering nomads who fought with the settled population.

Their rule in Iran was threatened by an ancient kingdom southeast of the Caspian Sea called Parthia. The Seleucid dynasty came to an end in 250 B.C. when Parthian armies invaded Iran. Arsaces became king, founding a Parthian dynasty. Future Parthian rulers extended the empire to include lands from Armenia to India.

THE SASANID DYNASTY

Parthian rule lasted for about 500 years. They established a large empire during this period, but it was constantly invaded by the Romans and by Afghan tribes. Civil wars further weakened the empire. Then, in A.D. 224, a Persian named Ardashir overthrew the Parthians and once again Iran was ruled by Persians under the Sasanid dynasty. IranShahr became the official name of the empire of Iran during the Sasanid dynasty.

Despite harassment from the Romans, the Sasanids managed to regain lost lands that were once part of the Achaemenid Empire. They even ventured as far as Istanbul, capital of the Eastern Roman Empire, but this proved to be a fatal mistake. Not only were the Persians defeated, they also had to withdraw from all the territories they had conquered.

In the name of Allah, zealous Arab invaders rose from the desert to spread the word of God and left a lasting legacy for Iran.

MOSLEM IRAN

Arab armies invaded Iran soon after Islam was founded by Mohammed in A.D. 622, and the Sasanid Empire collapsed. The coming of Islam had a profound influence on the Persians. It signified a decisive break with the past. The Persians found the Moslem religion more attractive than Zoroastrianism, the country's religion, and most Persians embraced Islam over a period of time. The Arabic language became the cultural language of Iran and a large number of Arabic words entered the Persian language. Even today, Persians use the Arabic script.

Arab power remained for nearly 600 years. During this period, famous Persians like Omar Khayyam brought glory to the Persian civilization. Persian culture became popular and spread beyond its borders. Europeans enjoyed Persian literature and music, studied its science and also appreciated Persian rugs and paintings.

A tomb left behind by one of the many invaders of Iran.

MONGOL ATTACKS

This Islamic empire came to an end with the devastating attacks of the Mongol hordes under Genghis Khan who struck terror into people. Iran did not escape the terrible sack of its cities and the massacre of whole populations. Hulagu, the grandson of Genghis Khan, finally put an end to the last caliphate in 1258 and founded the Il Khan dynasty. The Mongols ruled over a vast area which included Iran, Iraq and Anatolia as well as the Caucasus region. A later descendant of Hulagu converted to Islam and broke away from the Mongol empire of China.

After 1335, the Mongol empire in Iran broke up and Iran went through a period of several minor dynasties. Timur (also known as Tamerlane and a descendant of Genghis Khan) tried to establish Mongol rule again, but it did not last for long.

THE SAFAVID DYNASTY

Once again the Persians managed to reinstate their own power through the Safavid dynasty in 1502. The Safavids were a Turkish tribe. Their most famous ruler was Shah Abbas. Under his rule Iran prospered.

Shah Abbas reorganized the army with the advice of an English adventurer named Robert Sherley. With the help of his army, the Shah was able to stop invasions by Ottoman Turks as well as the various tribes that constantly raided the country. His greatest achievements, however, were in the arts.

Persian architecture reached new heights of beauty under the patronage of Shah Abbas. He built a magnificent city called Isfahan which he made the

capital of his empire. Travelers from the court of Queen Elizabeth I in England brought back glowing accounts of the beauty and splendor that was Persia. So magnificent was the charm of the city, it gave rise to the saying *Esphahan nesf-e-jehan* meaning "Isfahan is half of the world."

The Safavid dynasty suffered the same fate as other dynasties when Afghans invaded the country and captured Isfahan. However, the Afghan interlude was short-lived.

Nader Shah, a Turkish tribesman, not only drove the Afghans out, but later went on to conquer Afghanistan itself! Short of money, he decided to invade North India to capture the precious stones and jewelry he knew were kept in Delhi. He was not disappointed. The booty he brought back to Iran gave him the wealth he needed to make his empire viable. Among his booty was the Koh-i-Noor diamond and the famous Peacock Throne which was encrusted with precious stones of tremendous value.

In 1747, Nader Shah was assassinated. This was followed by a period of civil war between rival factions: the Zands and the Qajars ("KO-jars"). The latter emerged victorious and established the new Qajar dynasty.

The last absolute monarch in Iran was Shah Mohammed Ali of the Qajar Dynasty. He was forced to abdicate in 1909 after an uprising in the city of Tabriz.

THE QAJARS

During the 19th century, Iran was reluctantly involved in the political quarrels and colonial intrigues of Europe. Iran's strategic location was part of the problem. It lay between two warring nations—Great Britain and Russia. Russia, whose ports are frozen in winter and spring, was anxious to gain entry to the warm waters of the Caspian Sea, while Britain was anxious about any threat to the most important part of its empire— India. The Qajar rulers needed finance badly and granted concessions to Russia and Great Britain in return for loans. The conditions of these loans gave these major powers significant control over the internal affairs of Iran.

Many Iranians came into contact with the Western world. When they traveled overseas to attend universities, they came back with revolutionary ideas. They wanted changes to raise the level of development in Persia. A wave of popular demands resulted in the ruling Shah proclaiming a constitution in 1906.

In the meantime, the Russians and English decided to carve Iran into three zones, one under Russian influence, another under British influence and a third to remain neutral. The Iranians were furious, but could do nothing because they were heavily indebted to these two countries.

During World War I, Iran appealed to other nations to respect its neutrality, but both British and Russian troops used Iran as a short cut to the war zones. The Russian Revolution of 1917 finally resulted in an Iran-Soviet Russia Treaty of Friendship, with Russia withdrawing from Iran altogether. In 1921, with British support, a military officer called Reza Khan seized power in Tehran, deposed the Qajar Dynasty and crowned himself ruler or Shah of the new Pahlavi dynasty.

THE PAHLAVI DYNASTY

Reza Khan embarked on a program of modernization. In 1935, the name of the country was officially changed from Persia to Iran. He instituted many reforms, introducing civil law, encouraging the tribes to make permanent settlements, establishing the first national bank and outlawing the veil to achieve equality for women. The Shah tried to keep away from European politics and hired American financial advisers. He also encouraged ties with Germany.

It was his external policies which got Reza Shah into trouble. Iran's strategic location, as a bridge between Europe and Asia, and its oil resources led the British and Soviets to invade and occupy Iran in August 1941. The Shah's army was easily defeated. Reza Shah was forced into exile, abdicating his throne in favor of his son, Mohammed Reza.

The founder of the Pahlavi dynasty in 1926, Reza Shah.

Opposite: **By 1978, opposition to the Shah reached a feverish pitch. Demonstrators poured into the streets of Tehran and Qom demanding the return of Ayatollah Khomeini.**

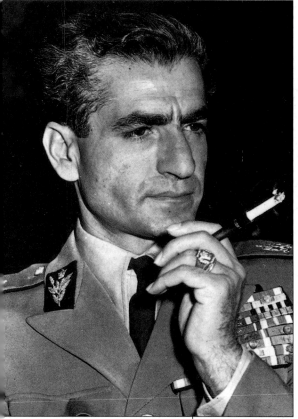

Above: **The last Shah of Iran, Mohammed Reza Shah.**

The young Shah had a difficult task trying to balance the interests of an emerging world power, the United States, against Iran's traditional enemies, Britain and Russia. He also faced opposition from nationalist groups who were not impressed with his government. The secret police agency known as SAVAK was set up to persecute all opponents of the Shah.

Despite the many reforms, opposition to the Shah's rule grew more intense. Iranian students overseas organized anti-Shah groups. Articles were written attacking the excesses of the Shah's personal lifestyle and corruption in the government. There was rapid industrial growth, but agriculture had declined to such an extent that 35% of the food was being imported. The Islamic clergy were also unhappy with the many reforms and the curbs to their power. There was much unrest in tribal areas.

THE REVOLUTION

Support for a religious leader, Ayatollah Khomeini ("ho-MAY-nee"), grew as Iran increasingly came under Western influence which many Iranians considered an insult to Islam. Though the country was rich, the people still remained poor as inflation set in. Many Iranians placed the blamed on the United States for supporting the Shah. The late 70s were filled with civil unrest and demonstrations. The Shah had no choice but to flee the country in 1978.

When Ayatollah Khomeini took over the country in February 1979 and proclaimed it an Islamic Republic, he declared that he would rid Iran of all Western influences. Iranian women were ordered to veil themselves again.

Severe punishments were introduced against anybody who broke the strict Islamic codes of behavior.

Many upper- and middle-class people fled the country to settle overseas. The country went through a very difficult period as the economy fell apart and unemployment rose. Ethnic unrest involving the Kurds and other minorities erupted in the northwest. There was a dramatic drop in the production of Iranian oil causing a panic in heavily industrialized countries.

Anti-Western feeling was further illustrated in the Iranian-hostage crisis when some Iranian students stormed the U.S. Embassy in Tehran and took 52 hostages. The United States made every effort to get their citizens back but the Ayatollah would only do this if Iranian assets frozen in the United States were released. The hostages were finally returned in January 1981.

A great revolution is never the fault of the people but of the government.
—Goethe

Captured Iranian soldiers under guard in an Iraqi war camp.

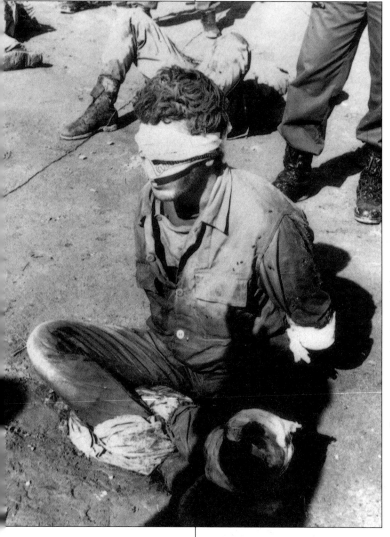

THE IRAN—IRAQI WAR

Tensions had always existed between Iran and its neighbor, Iraq, over religion—each country belonged to a different sect of Islam—and over ethnic differences as there are diverse ethnic groups living in each country.

The excuse that triggered the war was a border dispute over a front of 500 miles between Iran and Iraq. It was an opportune time for Iraq to attack as Iran was weakened by internal political problems. Fighting broke out in September 1980 and continued until 1988 with much loss of life and resources on both sides. Kurdish guerillas took advantage of the situation to fight for their self-determination and tried to gain control of parts of northern Iraq with the help of Iran.

The war finally ended in 1988, but in June 1989, another tragedy struck Iran. Their beloved leader Ayatollah Khomeini died of a heart attack. Amidst country-wide mourning a new ruler was proclaimed. His name is Ali Khamenei. He has vowed to continue the Islamic revolution.

IRANGATE

Irangate was the name given to a political scandal in the United States involving the secret sale of weapons to Iran in 1985, violating U.S. government policy. At a time when the United States was calling for a worldwide ban on sending arms to Iran, it had used the profits from a secret trade in arms to help the contra guerillas in Nicaragua. The arms were believed to have been sold to Iran via Israel.

Iranian protesters marching with an effigy of President Ronald Reagan, in a wave of anti-U.S. hysteria. The Iranians blamed the U.S. for supporting the Shah and for introducing anti-Islamic culture into the country.

GOVERNMENT

THE CONSTITUTION OF 1906 spelled out that the government of Iran was to consist of two chambers, one being the parliament called the Majlis-e-Shoray-e Mell, and the other the Senate, which consisted of 60 members. Since the toppling of the Shah and the proclamation of the Islamic Republic in 1979, only one chamber, the Majlis, remains. The 270 members of the Majlis are elected for a four-year term by the general population. Voting rights begin from the age of 16.

POWER STRUCTURE

The 1906 constitution was influenced by Western notions of parliamentary organization. In theory, the legislative power lies in the hands of the Majlis. The secular head of the nation is the president, and the executive is vested in the Council of Ministers headed by the prime minister and run by 24 ministers. A Guardian Council, comprising jurists and theologians, functions as a guardian of the constitution and it approves presidential candidates. At the provincial level, power rests with the governors. There are 24 provinces in all which are further subdivided into 195 districts.

Opposite: **The prime minister of Iran, Rafsanjani, was elected as the new head of state after Khomeini's death in 1989. Rafsanjani's election signified a more progressive and pragmatic era especially in trade and foreign policy.**

Below: **The meeting of the Majlis, or Islamic Consultative Assembly. The Majlis is the legislative body of the country and its representatives are elected by the people for a four-year term.**

The Senate in Tehran, Iran. The Majlis meets here to debate and legislate.

Since 1979, a number of new formulations and Islamic concepts of rule, have created a maze of overlapping functions and areas of power. The leadership of Iran is now in the hands of a spiritual leader called the *wali faqi*. The president is merely a figurehead. The *wali faqi* is chosen by a body called an Assembly of Experts. In 1989, another two bodies were created.

One was the Command Headquarters which now controls the army, the Revolutionary Guard and part of the police. The other is called the Expediency Council which was originally devised as a mediator between the Majlis and the Guardian Council. Its composition, including some of the most powerful men in Iran, has made it an influential body and it is said to dominate the Assembly of Experts, the Majlis, the General Command Headquarters, the Minister of Interior and the Secretariat of Friday Prayer Leaders.

THE WALI FAQI: SPIRITUAL LEADER OF IRAN

The most powerful person in the nation is the *wali faqi*, the spiritual leader of Iran. The *wali faqi* is officially chosen or approved by the Assembly of Experts, a committee consisting of 83 theologians who have the power to appoint, advise or even dismiss a leader. The interests of the *wali faqi* are represented by a Secretariat of Friday Prayer Leaders, a powerful group of theologians who disseminate the ideas of the *wali faqi*.

The *wali faqi* is considered to be the representative of the Imam (prophet) under Shiite doctrine. Vested with religious authority, he has power over all executive, legislative and military matters.

INDIVIDUAL POLITICIANS

Ayatollah Khomeini was the first *wali faqi* of the Islamic Republic. Indeed, the revolution that had brought about the fall of the Shah was called in his name. His vision of a new Islamic order, freed from Western influence, was partly successful due to his charisma. Khomeini's intention to turn Iran back into a strictly religious society was put into practice despite misgivings by the clergy.

At the time of the revolution, many of his contemporaries shared Khomeini's anti-Americanism which found vivid expression in posters and slogans.

Before his death, Khomeini had chosen a successor for the position of *wali faqi*, Ayatollah Hossein Ali Montazeri. However, Ayatollah Montazeri declined the post as he felt the responsibility of the position was too great. One day after Khomeini's death, the Council of Experts voted in the president, Hojatolislam Seyed Ali Khamenei, as Iran's new spiritual leader. Hojatolislam Hashemi Ali Akbar Rafsanjani, the speaker of the Majlis and commander-in-chief of the armed forces was elected as the head of state.

The *wali faqi* and leader of the Islamic Republic of Iran, Ayatollah Khamenei.

31

Celebrations to mark the sixth anniversary of the Islamic Revolution which saw the fall of the Shah and the end to monarchy in Iran. In its place, Khomeini introduced his ideas on Islamic political leadership led by religious leaders and intellectuals.

Since Rafsanjani's election in 1989, Iran has entered a more stable period of government, introducing some liberalization in politics and a gradual reinstatement of international ties. One of Rafsanjani's first official functions in August 1989 was to dismiss the Minister for Interior, Mohtashemi, who had been one of Rafsanjani's most ardent political opponents, especially in the area of foreign policy. Rafsanjani has sought to improve relations with the West, particularly the United States. He also admitted in 1990 that present Iranian laws are far stricter than the Koran demands, signaling a liberalization of some legal practices.

AYATOLLAH KHOMEINI

Ruhollah Musawi Hendi Khomeini was born in 1900 in Khomein and trained as a clergy-man in the holy city of Qom. In the 1930s, he became one of the leaders in the opposition to Reza Shah. In 1964, the Shah exiled him from Iran. Khomeini fled to Iraq and in 1978 to France. From exile he organized the opposition to the Shah which in 1979 led to the successful overthrow of the monarchy. Khomeini then became the unquestioned leader of Iran.

In all areas of life Khomeini ensured that the teachings of the Koran would be followed to the letter. This often required dramatic change in institutions, in everyday life, as well as

in domestic and foreign policy. This resulted in many new laws which were sometimes stricter than the Koran had prescribed. The 80s witnessed executions of religious and political opponents and the war with Iraq from 1980-1988. The war killed many Iranians and also severely harmed the economy.

A few months before his death, Khomeini made world headlines again when he pronounced the death sentence over writer and critic Salman Rushdie. Rushdie had written a novel called *Satanic Verses*, a controversial interpretation of some verses in the Koran. Khomeini's strictly religious, anti-modern, and militantly anti-American stance found many supporters within Iran. Khomeini maintained his power unchallenged until his death on June 3, 1989.

PARTIES

The last election of 1988 attracted only individual candidates. The only remaining and strictly religious party, the Islamic Republican Party was dissolved in 1987. It had provided 249 seats of the 270 in parliament in the 1984 elections. However, there are still Iranian parties, largely working from exile, and some mild opposition within Iran.

Many of the left-wing movements had helped in toppling the Shah, but were later prohibited and exiled because of clashes with funda- mentalist groups and the clergy. Among them were the Fedayeen-e Khalq (People's Fighters), the Mujaheddin-e Khalq (People's Holy Warriors) and Tudeh, the original Communist Party of Iran which was officially banned in 1983, and Kurdish parties. Among the more moderate opposition are various resistance movements working from outside Iran, such as the National Council of Resistance for Liberty and Independence and the National Resistance Movement. The latter, under Reza Pahlavi, the Shah's son, has called for a return to constitutional monarchy.

Within Iran, the foremost remaining legal opposition is the Nelzat-Azadi (Freedom Movement) which has repeatedly called for freedom of the press, speech and assembly. The slogans of the revolution in 1979 were "*Azadi, Esteqlal, Jumhori-ye Eslami*" (Freedom, Independence, Islamic Republic). Some of the goals have yet to be realized and it will be up to the present regime to adapt to contemporary needs.

HOJATOLISLAM HASHEMI ALI AKBAR RAFSANJANI

Rafsanjani was born in 1935 and was a pupil of Ayatollah Khomeini beginning in late childhood. He is arguably the most popular clergy-man in Iran today. Hundreds of thousands of people come to hear his sermons every Friday night. In his speeches he pronounces his political views. Rafsanjani has managed to maintain power so far despite fierce opposition from the radical mullahs for his liberalization programs. He maintains that he is following Khomeini's teachings and is putting these into practice. But he argues that times have changed, requiring different responses.

THE NATIONAL FLAG AND OFFICIAL EMBLEM OF THE ISLAMIC REPUBLIC OF IRAN

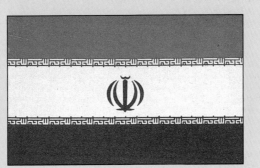

The Iranian national flag is made up of three colors, green on top, white in the middle and red at the bottom. The green and red strips are bordered with the slogan *Allah-o-Akhbar* meaning "Allah is the Greatest."

The emblem of the Islamic Republic of Iran is set in the center of the white strip and is red in color. It is a graphic representation of the word *Allah* and the words "There is no god but Allah."

ECONOMY

IRAN'S ECONOMIC DEVELOPMENT vastly accelerated in the last 40 years, giving rise to gigantic steel plants, oil refineries and factories. Its economy suffered greatly as a result of the Iran-Iraq war, reducing oil production by about 50% and causing inflation that, at times, ran as high as 400%. Signs of recovery appeared after the end of the war in 1988. Iran is rich in oil and natural gas, and is largely self-sufficient in its basic food supplies. Daring irrigation projects have made a vast difference to agricultural output, and they have ensured a yield in areas where there were once deserts. Dams are key to providing power to industry and water to agriculture.

AGRICULTURE

Within Iran, agriculture plays a major role even though only 10% of the countryside is suitable for farming. Much of the arable land is to the north of Tehran while large stretches of the remaining country are very hot and arid because of lack of rain. Iran is also covered by high mountains and rugged territory. It looks picturesque, but growth of vegetation is sparse because of the high altitude and the harsh, long winters.

Today, more land is being utilized for agriculture compared to 30 years ago because of the many dams that now dot the Iranian landscape.

Opposite: **Weaving the famous Persian carpet on an upright loom. Each carpet may take as long as six months to a year to complete and fetch very high prices in the market.**

Above: **Harvesting grain in Azerbaijan district in the northern tip of Iran. Farming in Iran is difficult as much of the work is still done without mechanization and farmers must depend on beasts of burden.**

Of the country's livestock, sheep are by far the most numerous, followed by goats, cattle, horses and mules.

Agriculture contributes 20% to Iran's economy and engages 39% of its labor force. Most of the country's crops, which include fruit, nuts, cereals, vegetables, sugar beet, rice, tobacco, gum, wool, cotton, silk, timber, tea and oilseeds, are grown in districts near the Caspian Sea, north of the capital, Tehran. Of these products the most important are rice and tea.

Livestock, mainly sheep, goats, cattle, donkeys, horses and camels, has also remained an important resource for Iran. Some animals are used for transport, others for plowing fields. Sheep, goats and cattle are used as food and yield other products such as wool, hides and milk.

Iran's access to the Caspian Sea and the Persian Gulf has resulted in an export fishing industry, particularly in caviar extracted from the sturgeon.

A modern oil refinery in the town of Abadan in southern Iran. Situated near the Persian Gulf, Abadan is a major oil refining and exporting center.

INDUSTRIES

Petroleum and natural gas account for most of the country's foreign income (98% of all export items) and over 80% of government revenue. Indeed, Iran holds the second largest deposits of natural gas in the world.

These industries are chiefly found in the southwest of Iran. The transport of natural gas and oil is increasingly through pipelines. One such pipeline runs for 682 miles through the west of Iran towards the Soviet Union, another goes to the Turkish port of Iskenderun on the Mediterranean Sea. Oil refining centers are found in Abadan and Kermanshah.

Gas and oil are not the only natural resources in Iran. Other minerals of great value to the economy include oil, copper, coal, iron ore, lead, zinc, salt and turquoise.

The abundance of natural resources has given rise to industrial and manufacturing companies. Steel production, for instance, has led to car manufacture, formerly in conjunction with French companies such as Citroen. In the stony arid plains between Tehran and Karaj, countless factories have been set up, chiefly in the textile, electrical and car industries.

An open-air carpet fair displays products made by the Turkomans. These fairs attract people from the surrounding villages and provide an opportunity for friends to meet and to entertain the family.

CARPET AND TEXTILE PRODUCTION

Persian carpet weaving has a very long history. Carpets have always been used for prayer and, for centuries, they were often the only furniture in a house or dwelling. Nomads used carpets as doors to their tents and also laid them on the floor for sitting and sleeping. Some very valuable carpets have been found, said to date back as far as 500 B.C.

The carpet industry was revived in the late 19th century and then quickly became the main export earner, leading to the growth and spread of small workshops throughout Persia.

In modern Iran, the industry received new impetus when Reza Shah founded the National Carpet Company in Tehran, with thousands of workshops created throughout Iran. Today, Persian carpets from Hamadan are among the best-known carpets in the world.

REGIONAL PRODUCTION

Apart from the famous Persian carpet, there are other beautiful traditional handicrafts. Hamadan is renowned for its pottery and leather works. Bakhtaran, the largest city of western Iran, produces knitted footwear. From Gorgan and Mashhad come the dresses, tunics and blouses made from natural silk, known as *kalaghe*, Astrakhan bonnets, and embroidered sheepskin coats.

The Khorasan mine in Mashhad produces turquoise which is worked into all kinds of jewelry. Timber is rare in Iran, and hence woodwork and wooden items are not high on the crafts list. One can find some carved items and wooden kitchen tools around the Caucasian mountains and near the Caspian Sea. Pottery, ceramics and glasswork, however, can be found throughout Iran, and pottery, especially, has experienced a recent revival and renaissance led by the National Crafts School in Tehran.

THE ART OF CARPET WEAVING

Carpet weaving is a highly skilled and laborious craft. It may take as long as a year or two to finish one carpet by the traditional method of a knotted stitch, performed on a knotting loom which is a simple frame. There are two main kinds of stitches, a Turkish knot done with a needle and a Persian knot, without needle, which is used for very fine carpets.

One square yard of high quality carpet may have up to one million knots, and an average carpet about 200,000. A very skilled worker can average about 12,000 knots a day.

When the carpet is finished it has to go through two more processes: crushing the fibers so that the carpet is pliable, and washing and drying. In some areas, such as Rey near Tehran, these processes have become a tourist attraction.

TRADING IN THE BAZAAR

Much of modern Iranian trade is conducted in the manner of Western industrialized countries. Business is done in offices and shops, by telephone and fax machines, while goods are distributed on trucks, trains, ships and planes. But one feature that gives Iranian trade a local color is the bazaar.

Though there are air-conditioned shopping centers in the cities, bazaars are still important places for selling and buying goods. Street bazaars are usually under cover of canvas or firmer structures to provide protection from the sun, the wind and weather. The bazaars in the present capital city Tehran, and in a former capital city, Isfahan, are particularly famous and picturesque.

FOREIGN TRADE

The Iranian Revolution, followed by the Iran-Iraq War, had devastating effects on the Iranian economy and the country's international debts grew during this period. Because the Koran has the least specific advice on economic matters, debates on what a truly Islamic economy should be are common. Traditional mullahs are against any reform, but Rafsanjani, who is considered a pragmatist, is likely to steer a moderate course.

Foreign trade, particularly the export of oil and gas, gradually returned to normal after 1984-85, slowly increasing throughout the late 1980s. Apart from oil and natural gas, the chief export items of Iran are carpets and fruits.

Iran's major trading partners are Western industrialized countries, chief among them the United States, Japan and Italy, who play leading roles in Iran's export market. Imports come mainly from the Federal Republic of Germany and Japan, although some also come from the United Kingdom and Italy. In 1982, attempts were made to nationalize foreign trade, but the Guardian Council then ruled that such a proposal was against Islamic principles and the idea was rejected.

There has been increasing trade and economic collaboration with Eastern Europe including the former Soviet Union, Romania, Czechoslovakia and Hungary. Under trade agreements, these countries barter food for oil and provide expertise for agricultural and technological development in Iran.

The sturgeon is found in the Caspian Sea. The sturgeon's most valuable resource is its roe, or eggs, which are made into caviar and exported.

IRANIANS

ACCORDING TO THE 1986 CENSUS, Iran has a population of about 52 million. All Iranians, regardless of ethnic background, have a strong sense of family and clan. In each society, people group themselves into social patterns that have evolved for distinct reasons. Climate, economy, density of population and religion play a role in the way social life is structured.

In Iran, and in much of the Middle East, people from the harsh conditions of semi-desert and desert environments live and group together differently than those from the lush, fertile coastal areas and valleys.

Opposite: **A Turkoman welcomes you to his village. The hospitality of the Iranians is partly due to the harsh land and fragile lifestyle which makes people more dependent on each other.**

Left: **A nomadic campsite. Each tent is surrounded by a fence to keep out wild animals and to protect the family from the desert winds. The tents and fences are collapsible and easily mounted on horses when moving in search of pastures and towns.**

TRIBES, CLANS AND FAMILIES

Among nomads, the tribe is the basic unit. It is ruled by a tribal chief. There are elaborate customs dictating behavior, line of authority and marriage patterns. There are also tribal villages indicating that a nomadic group has recently settled down. Nomads, in general, consider themselves superior to villagers, so they will always acknowledge their nomadic background and ancestry.

In villages, the most important social groups are the clans and the family. The family comes first and loyalty to it is important in daily life, and even for survival. A clan consists of several interrelated families that usually mingle

The traditional costume of the Kurds reminds us of the gypsies that roam the breadth of Europe.

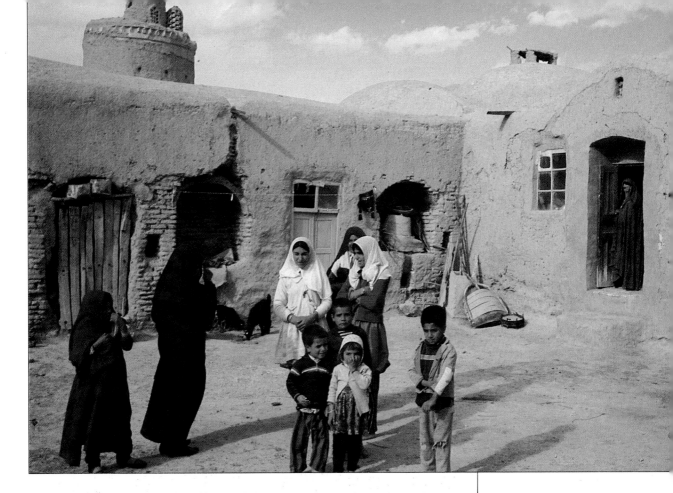

in daily life, work together and share whatever good fortune or bad luck comes their way.

Many villages in Iran consist of just one clan; larger ones may have several. Thus, village groups are tightly knit and have a strong sense of belonging.

In cities, tribes and clans have lost almost all importance. Instead, in cities, we speak of extended families—a network of uncles, aunts and cousins. People may not always live together under the same roof anymore, but they do take each other's concerns and life very seriously.

Families used to be very large. But as health care improves and living standards rise, the average size of a family has decreased over time. The number of children per family in Iran, averaging about six, is still extraordinarily high when compared to the Western world, but it is in fact lower than in most other Middle East countries.

Around the vast courtyard, many mud-brick rooms are found. Each room may house a whole family.

Above: **A chieftain's wife of the Qashqa'i tribe parades the wealth of her community. The Qashqa'i tribe is found in the area around Shiraz, in the southwest of Iran.**

Opposite: **A Bakhtiari man and his wife. The Bakhtiari tribe settled in the Zagros Mountains and live mainly as shepherds.**

Iranians have maintained a strong sense of family even when, for some of them, life has become relatively Westernized. They visit each other often, family meals are taken together at night and there is time for lengthy conversations.

In a strictly Islamic family, divisions exist by gender. For instance, there are areas of a house where only women can be and others where only men can be. In such strict environments, men usually seek out each other's company for conversation rather than their wives and children. Since the revolution in 1979, polygamy has been on the rise. Moslem law allows a man to take four wives. For a man, divorce is very easy: all he has to do is say "I divorce you" three times. He must then give to the wife whatever is hers under the marriage contract.

A shy little Persian girl.

ETHNIC GROUPS

Iran is a multi-ethnic society. It consists of Iranians, Azerbaijanis, Kurds, Arabs, Turkomans, Baluchis ("ba-LOO-chees"), Jews, the Qashqa'i ("kosh-kah-EE") and some Westerners. Ethnic unrest was widespread around the time of the revolution. Iranians account for about 66% of the population, the Azerbaijanis for about 20%, Kurds make up about 5% and Arabs 4%. The remainder are a mixture of foreigners, tribal groups and nomads.

PERSIANS The Iranians are an Indo-Germanic people who are believed to have migrated from Central Asia to the Middle East around 2000 B.C. The history of the Persians, as we have already seen, shows that the Persian people belong to an ancient culture. At times, Persia was a very powerful country whose territory spread as far as India. The monuments of the Persian past can still be seen throughout the country. Iranians are proud of their past and their history. Renaming Persia as Iran in 1934 was a way of saying that the ancient Persia was going to be a modern country, with its roots fully acknowledged. It is important to remember that Iranians are not Arabs. They have their own distinct ethnic profile. What makes Iranians part of the Middle East is the common religion of Islam they share. But even so, Iran has its own beliefs that distinguish it from other Middle Eastern nations.

ARABS Iran has a relatively large Arabic population. Many Arabs are concentrated in the southern province of Khuzestan. Because there are so many Arabs here, some neighboring Arab-speaking states do not regard this region as being part of Iran.

On Syrian and Iraqi maps the area is still referred to as Arabestan. The Khuzestan province is important to the Iranian government because it is rich in oil deposits. Ethnic conflict has flared up occasionally. During the 1979 revolution, the Arabs demanded a greater share of the oil revenue, local autonomy and an end to discrimination. Arabs in Iran feel they are not getting their fair share of income or employment, or in politics.

Many Iranian boys keep their hair short to beat the heat.

OTHER MINORITIES There are other minority groups which have repeatedly made bids for autonomy. There were autonomy movements in Azerbaijan, Baluchistan and Kurdistan. Many minorities supported the revolution of 1979 because they hoped that the removal of the Shah would improve their own position in Iran. It did not. Khomeini continued the Shah's trend to centralize power and invest ultimate authority in the government, with one important difference: it abolished democratic representation of various groups and peoples.

The Azerbaijani and the Kurds are indeed, major groups. Together they account for 25 % of the Iranian population. Kurds have the problem that their people are spread over several countries, such as Iran, Iraq and Turkey. Azerbaijanis, by contrast, are a well-defined group which predominates in one area. Nevertheless, the Kurds have managed to maintain their own language, religion and, socially, to keep to themselves.

A Kurdish mother prepares her daughter for a long journey.

NOMADIC PEOPLES

We only have estimates of the number of nomads and semi-nomadic people living in Iran. It is estimated that they constitute about 3 % to 4 % of Iran's population and some claim that the number is as high as 10%. This variation is partly accounted for by the way nomads are classified. Some move around their entire lives, some confine themselves to a set path and a set area, yet others are semi-permanent and have established homesteads

A Baluchi man weaving cord from some leaves.

in several locations. Most of the nomads are organized in tribes, like the Bakhtiari, Baluchi, Lurs, Kurds and Khamseh. Politically, the role of nomads has not been an easy one. Every Iranian ruler in the past has tried to harness nomadic tribes and to get them to settle in specific areas. This move has only been partially successful.

Over the last two centuries, one group in particular, has acquired some political significance. These are the Qashqa'i who formed their own confederacy. In the emerging modern state of Iran, the existence of subgroups, such as the Qashqa'i with their own laws, leaders and independence, was seen as a threat. In 1979, several leaders (called khans) of the Qashqa'i returned from exile once they knew the Shah had been overthrown. They generally commanded authority among the Iranian people. Some of them became very popular and charismatic leaders in the revolution of 1979. Initially, they supported Khomeini who, in turn, was not quite as generous to the Qashqa'i. Years before, he had regarded them as feudal barons and highway robbers.

Through desert and mountain passes, these nomads travel along a traditional route which will provide sufficient water and shelter until they reach a more permanent campsite.

Khomeini crushed the political power of the Qashqa'i once the revolution was won. In 1982, small groups of Qashqa'i, barricaded in the mountains of southwest Iran, still defended themselves against Khomeini's Revolutionary Guard.

Even today, with the ever increasing influence of government and the pervasive influence of modern economics, the nomads of Iran are largely self-sufficient. Men hunt and tend the herds. The herds provide them with food and milk, supply hair or wool for spinning, and hides for use as tents.

Women spin their own yarn and weave clothes for themselves and for the rest of the tribe. They also make rugs. Some of the most beautiful rugs are in fact made by nomadic tribes. They use these rugs as flooring for their tents or as windshields against the sand.

The proverb, "where thy carpet lies is thy house," has true meaning in nomadic life. Most nomads get by without using money. The few goods they want they barter for in town markets. They exchange rugs, butter or milk for other goods.

In a traditional costume that reminds us of the civilization of ancient Persia, a Qashqa'i girl performs a whirling dance during a tribal festivity.

LIFESTYLE

BY 6 A.M. THE CITY IS ALREADY AWAKE and alive with the hustle and bustle of day. One can see people on the streets selling hot cups of tea and newspapers. The reason for the early morning activity is because the working day starts early. Factories begin operations between 7 a.m. and 7:30 a.m. and schools start at 8 a.m. Working days are usually eight hours long.

Common to all work practices in Iran is an extended lunch break. In government offices, schools, universities and factories, it is usual to have two hours off for lunch. Some people go to restaurants and then take a nap in the streets or in the park. In the very hot summer months, some lunch breaks may be even longer. But people then work later into the evening.

Most Iranians go home and have lunch with their families. Thus, families see each other during the day and family activities are not confined only to the evening hours.

For those who are self-employed, the working day is usually longer, typically 10 hours a day. They, too, take their extended lunch break, but this often extends to four hours in the middle of the day as shops tend to stay open until 10 p.m. so that customers can shop after work.

In Iran, Friday is the day of prayer. Government offices and schools are closed on Thursday afternoons and Fridays. Self-employed people must close their shops and rest from their work for at least half a day.

Opposite: **Two Iranian women go about their daily chores in the countryside.**

Above: **Breakfast in the morning consists of tea, milk and bread that is freshly baked.**

As piped water has not reached many of the villages in Iran, rural folks still wash their clothes in the rivers and wells.

COUNTRY LIFE

In the country, life's rhythm is dictated by the seasons and the times of day. Most villages do not have electricity, heating or pumped water. The working day begins when the sun has risen and finishes when the sun goes down. Oil lamps may provide some light in the evening, but this is not good enough for spinning, weaving or carpet making. Water has to be carried from the common village well, and the herds and fields have to be tended. Children help their parents and begin work early, too, unless they go to school. The more traditional a village is, the more likely it is self-sufficient.

Most of the work is hard because it is based entirely on manual labor. Few villages have tractors. Some others have animals for plowing. In areas such as the Yazd and Isfahan regions, the farmer has to plow, irrigate, weed, reap and thresh without the help of machines or animals.

EDUCATION

In the 1960s, Iran underwent a large-scale educational reform and many schools were built. From 1967 to 1968, 67 teacher-training schools and eight universities were founded.

Much effort was made to teach people to read and write. By 1968, 35,000 "Literacy Corps" teachers had been trained, and they went out to teach adults and primary schoolchildren. Illiteracy in Iran then stood around 70%. Now it stands at around 50%. Literacy is high in the cities but low in the rural areas. For example, when the International Labour Organization (ILO) examined the effect of the Literacy Corps, it found that enrollment in primary school stood at 39% in rural areas compared to 90% in the cities.

Khomeini's policies have not helped to reduce illiteracy because, in his view, women do not need training and schooling. Before the revolution, only 34% of all girls attended primary school, and even fewer went on to university. The illiteracy rate among girls is likely to be on the increase again.

Primary school for children between the ages of 6 to 12 is compulsory in Iran, but not all parents send their children to classes. This is either because the schools are too far away or because they need the children to work in the family business or on the farm. Many children who do not go to school are therefore not idle. They work instead.

Happy schoolgirls going home after class. Schools in Iran are segregated according to sex in keeping with Islamic beliefs.

Secondary school is not compulsory and is generally free of charge. Students cannot go to high school automatically. They have to pass a major qualifying examination first. Secondary schools are very strict and demand total academic devotion. Every high school year finishes with major examinations. Should a student fail one subject (out of as many as 12) he or she will have to repeat the entire year.

The school week in Iran starts on Saturday morning at 8 a.m. and finishes on Thursday at lunchtime. The school year begins in September and, except for a two-week holiday in March for the New Year, carries on until June the following year without a break. July and August, the hottest months of the year, are summer holidays.

Many poor families cannot afford to send their children to school although education at primary level is free. Sometimes, elderly fathers, such as this craftsman, need their help to make a living to feed the family.

EVERYDAY LIFE

As in most countries, city and country life have their own distinct rhythm. Perhaps the contrasts appear stronger in Iran than elsewhere because the country has traditions that, in some areas, have largely remained unchanged for over 1,000 years. The 1976 census found that there were 65,000 villages in Iran of which only 27% had more than 250 inhabitants. In these small communities, customs change very little and manage to coexist with modern technological changes.

The big cities in Iran are beautifully spacious and elegant. They are lined with trees and the pavements are bordered by an unbroken row of small shops that specialize in a variety of goods. In major cities, there are also modern supermarket complexes, usually several stories high.

One has to distinguish between two main types of cities. One is the traditional city and the other is the modern city. The traditional city is easily recognizable by three features. One is the mosque in the center, placed usually at the intersection of two major through roads. Such a central mosque is not just a place for prayer, but it also has a large courtyard so that people can get together for informal meetings and spontaneous gatherings.

Near the mosque one finds the government buildings or an old palace where a ruler used to live. Surrounding the mosque and palace are small streets branching out in all directions. At least one of them functions as the main bazaar of the city.

The city center is thus a hub of faith, of power, and trade. Streets tend to be very congested with people on their way to the mosque and markets, donkeys, livestock, produce and goods of all kinds. One writer, William O. Douglas, has described the very special atmosphere in these words:

Iranian women, in their traditional clothes, the *chador*, shop at a bazaar. The *chador* covers the body, hands, legs and face. Beneath it, the women wear a pair of long pants.

"The movement of the crowd through the bazaar has endless variety. Mullahs in white turbans and black gowns, Qashqa'is with felt hats having brims in front and behind, Bakhtiari with the tall, brimless black felt hat, turbaned camel drivers, merchants wearing sandals, flowing trousers, and Western shirts, old men with long black coats, young men in slacks and open shirts, barefooted urchins darting in and out …

"Apart from the movement of the crowd is the medley of voices and noises. Apart from them are the odors. We of the West have shut up all our odors in tin cans. The East has preserved them for the nostrils. Spices, tobacco, candies, camel dung, burros, people fill the bazaar with a pungent odor … It's a powerful force pulling one toward the East over and again."

In the modern city, much of that intimate atmosphere is gone. One of the main differences, compared to the traditional city, is that the modern cities are not people-centered. They are car-centered. In Tehran, boulevards are often eight lanes wide. In the business center, with its administrative buildings, its hotels, cinemas, restaurants and department stores, there is little that reminds one of what we knew as the Orient.

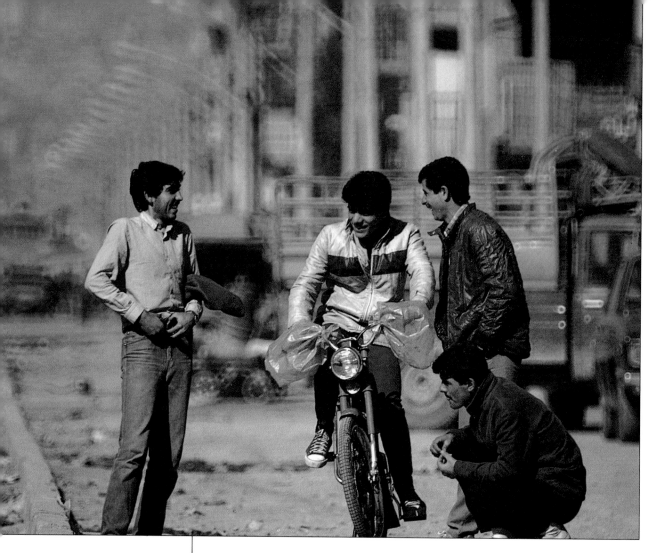

TRAFFIC

Despite the wide streets, city traffic tends to be congested, and it is not without dangers. Driving in Tehran can be a nightmare because drivers rarely let others know what they intend to do, and they do not always stop at traffic lights. The general frenzy, made very audible by a constant tooting of horns, causes countless chaotic traffic jams which, at times, take hours to unravel.

Driving in the country is much easier, though buses and herds of animals may slow the pace. Gravel roads are generally rutted and the distances between gasoline stations are long (62 miles or more apart). But there are also many paved highways on which travel is easy.

HOUSING

CITY LIFE There are a number of large cities in Iran where living costs can be extremely high. In Tehran, for example, a high school principal may earn 24,000 rials a month, an above average income, but may spend nearly 10,000 rials to rent a three-bedroom house. This represents nearly 50% of the total income.

Essentially, the housing problem is no different than in most Western countries. Most city people are neither very rich nor very poor, and they live in relatively modest accommodation. The issue of housing and crowding is made more difficult by the fact that families tend to be large. Children and parents often sleep in close proximity to one another.

The flow of population to the cities has created housing shortages, such as in Tehran, the capital of Iran.

COUNTRY LIFE In Iran nearly 39% of the population still work in agriculture and live in the villages. The problem of housing does not arise because many families usually own property. Yet, village accommodation does tend to be rather crowded.

A marked difference in style occurs further out in the country. In a hut, there is very little furniture as we know it. Rugs are either placed on the clay floor or hung as wall hangings. People sit on the floor to eat, chat and work.

THE VILLAGE

Largely because of a limited supply of timber or other building materials, and partly due to the climate, houses are usually made of mud bricks. Mud bricks are often regarded as the building material of the poor as it is cheap and readily available. Ninety percent of all village buildings in Iran are made of mud bricks.

Mud bricks help to cool the house in summer and keep it warm in winter. In addition, houses in desert or semi-desert areas usually have wind towers. These towers trap the wind and circulate the air to cool the house. Partly because of the heat and the possibility of sandstorms, village buildings are clustered together.

A large clay wall surrounds the village. Inside is a maze of small lanes leading to various houses. The outside village wall has several purposes. It protects the villagers from sandstorms and the cutting cold winds in winter, and it allows them to defend themselves against bandits. The walls also protect their inhabitants from the strong winds of Central Asia which can blow at 124 miles an hour and last for 120 days. These high walls are not found near the Caspian Sea where the plentiful vegetation prevents winds from gaining such destructive force.

The privacy of individual families is maintained by small enclosed

courtyards. There is often only one real street in the village, which has a
water channel or *djuba* built in the middle. This is the main water supply
and the lifeline for the entire village. Because of the position of the *djuba*,
it would be hard for an outsider to steal any of the water without being seen.
There is no piped water and no electricity in these villages. Many of them just
accommodate one family group of around 30 to 50 inhabitants.

The harsh conditions for survival—too little water and poor soil—make
it difficult to sustain larger groups. Farming in the Iranian countryside is very
hard work and many live at subsistence levels. The lure of better incomes
and better living conditions in the city has resulted in a migration of people
from the countryside.

A typical Iranian village
with its main street lined
by mud-brick houses in
the background.

OLD AGE

An elderly street vendor. For those who do not have children to look after them, taking care of themselves is a must as the state does not provide social security.

Life expectancy in Iran is still rather low—around 59 years as against the 70-plus years in most Western countries. This does not mean that people do not live to an old age, but in most cases, it indicates that infant mortality is high. In Iran, over 10% of live births do not survive as against the 1% or less in the developed nations.

An elderly street vendor. For those who do not have children to look after them, taking care of themselves is a must as the state does not provide social security.

There are no pension benefits and there is little welfare for the aged in Iran. Care for the old is entirely in the hands of the family. As extended family life is common, it is natural for the children to look after their aging parents and to fulfill their wishes and personal needs.

Iranian families do not perceive this as a burden but as a good responsibility. The old are highly respected, even venerated. They are seen as holding the key to wisdom and to family stability, and it is therefore regarded as proper and beneficial for Iranian families to live with and care for their aging relatives.

An extended Kurdish family in Kurdistan. The men are dressed in typical Kurdish clothes with long-sleeved cotton shirts, baggy pants and a cummerbund around the waist.

RELIGION

ISLAM IS THE YOUNGEST OF THE THREE WORLD RELIGIONS: Buddhism, Christianity and Islam. It is a very widespread religion, predominating in the Middle East, but practiced in Northern Africa, Pakistan and Indonesia. Significant numbers of Moslems also live in Albania, Yugoslavia, Central Asia, Malaysia, India, China and the Philippines.

Over 90% of all inhabitants in Iran are Moslems. The majority of Moslems belong to the Shiite sect while a small section of the population belong to the Sunni and Sufi group. There is a smattering of Jews, Parsees and Armenian Christians. Since the revolution in 1979, religion has not only become important, but it influences every aspect of daily life, customs, laws and government decisions. Iran is a religious-state, which means that its religious rules are synonymous with its state rules. In all matters it is the teachings of Islam, as interpreted by Khomeini and his followers, that determine state life, not the other way around.

Opposite: **Much personal time is spent in the mosques reading the Koran or in quiet prayer.**

Below: **Rising majestically above the surrounding buildings, the Royal Mosque of Isfahan is a tribute to the artistic glory of Persia and a testament to the faith of its people. It was built in the 17th century by Shah Abbas.**

LAWS OF ISLAM

Islam is a religion of laws. Every Moslem accepts that there is only one God. According to the Koran, the holy book of Islam, he is the creator of everything and is all-powerful. Islam believes in a day of judgement, when God will decide if people have been good or bad in life and either send them to hell or to paradise.

The Koran attempts to harness all areas of life into laws and obligations. It can therefore be said that the Koran provides guidelines for all aspects of life. It must be remembered that the Koran was written in the 7th century and some of the social rules and beliefs expressed are a reflection of the times in which it was written. But the Koran is not the only source of laws. Over the centuries, Islamic laws or *fikh* have evolved and changed. In the 8th century, the first comprehensive accounts of the Prophet Mohammed were collected. All his known sayings, his decisions, and his responses to life situations and to philosophical and legal questions were brought together in a book. This collection, known as Sunna ("SOON-na"), forms the other indispensable source for the Islamic faith and legal system.

Opposite: **In the city of Mashhad stands the shrine of Imam Reza Shah. Every year thousands of Shiite devotees make their pilgrimage to this shrine.**

A *sufi* clergy in prayer. The *sufis* belong to a minority sect of Islam.

SHIITE VS SUNNI

The main difference between the Shiites ("SHEE-ites") and the Sunnis ("SOON-nees") is that the Sunnis recognize the legitimate claim of successors (caliphs) who were not related to the Prophet. Shiites do not recognize this claim.

The rift between Sunnis and Shiites occurred early in Persian and Arabic history. One of the chief points of argument was what to do after the death of the Prophet Mohammed in A.D. 632. The Shiites argued that Imam Ali, the chief disciple of the Prophet, had the right to be regarded as the lawful heir and successor and that he was entitled to rule the Moslem community after the Prophet's death. Ali was seen by them as the only Moslem worthy to succeed the Prophet as a ruler.

But fights broke out and the group now called the Sunnis were the ones most strongly opposed to this claim. But with the establishment of a Sunni caliphate, the Arabic world quickly conquered new territory and expanded over time, gaining new converts along the way. Today, around 90% of all Moslems are Sunnis. Shiite Islam, though, is the national religion of Iran. Other differences between the Sunnis and Shiites evolved over time but the original dispute is still one of the most important differences.

Another important development in Islam was the religious mysticism called Sufism which spread in the 9th century.

ULEMAS, AYATOLLAHS AND MULLAHS

The Islamic religion claims not to have a hierarchy of authority and priesthood. However, the learned men (the ulema, ayatollah and mullah) have become unchallenged political, social and spiritual leaders.

Interpreting the Koran and all Islamic teachings has been a chief activity of its religious leaders. As in other world religions, such reinterpretation in the fast changing world of the 19th and 20th centuries brought new challenges. The question was how relevant religion was to modern life and how one could remain true to one's religion in the face of substantial social and economic changes.

A mullah on the streets of Isfahan. Much respect and recognition are given to these learned men as they are the teachers of Shiite Islam.

Opposite: Khomeini re-introduced strict Islamic laws, which curtailed the freedom of movement of women substantially and gave them very few rights. The re-introduction of the law of the *chador*, the full-length outer cloak, mostly in black, is only a symbol of the many social and legal changes that have occurred.

IMPACT OF RELIGIOUS LAWS IN IRAN

Immediately after the revolution, bans were placed on imported meat, luxury goods and alcohol. In 1980, music was condemned as a seducer that detracted Moslems from the more serious purpose of serving Allah. Cinemas, too, were temporarily closed down.

Any behavior or act which was regarded as morally dangerous had stiff penalties imposed upon it. For instance, alcohol consumption and homosexuality are now punishable by death. Adultery could lead to stoning in public. Kissing in public was punished by 100 lashes.

Though not all Iranians agree with these rules, there is no doubt that Islam unites all Iranians in general. The entire structure of everyday life revolves around making time for prayer and for contemplation. Shops are shut on Thursday afternoon and all day Friday, and even those businessmen who do not go to prayer will shut down their shop and close the blinds. Shiism in Iran underwent a profound transformation in the 1960s. As it became a political force which eventually helped to overthrow the last Shah, it also moved from being merely a religious belief to a way of life.

WOMEN AND ISLAM

Everywhere in Islam, there are strict gender divisions and women take a backstage in religious affairs. The religious revival of Iran had many implications for women.

Under Khomeini's rule, women do not own even the clothes they wear. They have no rights over their children, little or no protection against a violent husband. If he kills her, her family must pay a considerable price for his death sentence. If they cannot meet the cost, he goes free. A husband can order his wife out of the house, he can divorce her without even telling

her, and he can marry several wives.

Women have now been systematically pushed out of the work force. All women in public service have been forced into part-time work so that nothing hinders their holy duty of motherhood.

OTHER RELIGIONS AND SECTS

THE BAHA'I The Baha'i religion originated in Iran in the 19th century. It was started by an Iranian religious visionary, Mirza Ali Mohammed, who called himself the Bab, meaning "the gate." His follower, Mirza Husain Ali, was responsible for spreading the movement and gathering more believers. He took the title Baha Ullah meaning "Glory of God."

To Moslems, the Baha'is are traitors to the "true faith." The Baha'is believe the Messiah has already come. They criticize some of Mohammed's teachings as outmoded, for instance the legal inequalities of the sexes and of creeds, polygamy and the prejudice against music. Baha Ullah taught that religious truth is not absolute but relative, and that each age had to modify and adapt the teachings through new wisdoms. Particularly since the revolution of 1979, the Baha'i faith has not been tolerated in Iran. The religion has been prohibited and fought in every way. Despite the persecution, there are still some Baha'is living in Iran today.

THE GHULAT The Ghulat are an extremist Shiite sect. They are found not only in Iran, but also in Iraq, Syria and Turkey. They usually go by several names: Ahl-i Haqq (truth worshipers), Ali Ilahis (deifiers of Ali) or Ahl-i Allah (people of God).

As a sect they are very secretive. Their ceremonies are conducted at night in secluded surroundings, a practice dictated at times by the need to avoid persecution. But this has given rise to all sorts of myths about their rituals and beliefs. They meet every Thursday night and the first night of the lunar moon. Not unlike Christian religions, the Ghulat practice public and private confessions.

One visible difference from mainstream Shiites is the importance of the moustache. When Ali took instructions from the Prophet Mohammed, he is said to have cowered at his feet and his moustache brushed against the body of the Prophet. Thus Ali's moustache acquired holiness and, in allegiance to Ali, no Ghulat today ever clips his moustache.

Opposite above: **Abdul Baha was the son of Baha Ullah and successor to the leadership of the movement after his father's death.**

Opposite below: **A Baha'i temple, shaped like a lotus blossom.**

Above: **The Church of St. Thaddeus in Azerbaijan. Built high on a mountain pass, the church's architecture is a reminder of the Byzantine age when churches were constructed like fortresses to defend against attacks by Islamic armies.**

Below: **The Torah lies open in the tomb of Esther, the Jewish wife of Cyrus the Great. Esther is credited in the Bible as the queen responsible for getting Cyrus to free thousands of Jewish prisoners from the city of Babylon and allowing them to return to Palestine.**

Opposite: **A Zoroastrian village.**

CHRISTIANS, JEWS AND OTHERS There are also some Christians, Jews and Zoroastrians in Iran. Their numbers are relatively small and they do not play any political or important cultural role.

Most Christians, around 60,000 of them, are members of the Armenian Church. Their largest community lies in the Jolfa district at Isfahan. They even have their own cathedral, called the St. Savior Cathedral, which is allowed to celebrate Sunday Mass. Another Armenian religious center is St. Thaddeus with its fortified monastery in northern Azerbaijan. In July each year, thousands of Christian pilgrims come here to worship. Therefore, it is important to note that the Azerbaijani form an ethnic community that sets them quite firmly apart from the rest of Iran in language, area and partly in religion.

There are also some Jews in Iran, numbering around 150,000. They constitute 0.3% of the population. Since Khomeini's revolution, some have tried to leave Iran, but there are also ancient Jewish communities in Iran which have not changed much in lifestyle and custom since Babylonian times.

ZOROASTRIANISM

A truly Iranian group is the Zoroastrians. There are only 21,000 followers of this faith left, but those few tell of ancient Persian times. Zoroastrianism is the early Aryan faith.

It is built on the teachings of Ahura Mazda and the great philosopher Zoroaster. Zoroaster was a prophet and philosopher who lived probably around 600 B.C. He is said to have lived to the age of 77. But he did not die a natural death. He was burned to death because he had criticized the religious orgies and bloody animal sacrifices of the local inhabitants. As a religion, Zoroastrianism has almost died out.

LANGUAGE

LINGUISTS DISTINGUISH THREE FORMS of the Persian language: Old Persian, spoken and written by the Achaemedians between the 6th and 4th centuries B.C.; Middle Persian, spoken by the Sasanids between the 3rd and 7th centuries A.D.; and New Persian that broadly defines the language spoken and recorded since the 9th century. Persian is referred to as Farsi.

The name of the language and of the people comes from Pars, an area in the southwest of the Iranian highlands. The influence of Arabic eventually changed Pars to Fars. In ancient history, it was called Persis with the capital city of Persepolis. The people called themselves Irani, the Persian name for Aryan. In fact, *Iran* means literally "The land of the Aryans."

Farsi is an Indo-European language and belongs to a large family of languages which includes English, German and French. This also means that it is not at all related to Turkish or Arabic, even though the language is written in Arabic script.

Opposite: **The development of the Arabic script from simple lines to the ornate and breathtaking calligraphy we see today is a result of the artistic achievements of the Islamic world through the centuries. From rugs to mosques, Moslem artists have been decorating their work with the Arabic script praising Allah and his deeds.**

Below: **Adapting the Arabic script to include new words to meet modern scientific discoveries has proved to be a challenging but successful task for linguists, as this biology class demonstrates.**

NEW PERSIAN

New Persian is the oldest literary language known in the region. From the 9th century onwards, it was written in Arabic letters. The written language is very different from the spoken Farsi and mastered only by people with substantial education. It has remained basically unchanged since the 11th century and is based on the 50,000 couplets (two lines of a verse that usually rhyme), entitled *The Book of Kings* by a Persian poet, Ferdowsi, who narrated the history of Persia.

The art of writing is called calligraphy. Texts are written and read from

A blue ceramic tile adorned with flowers and Arabic calligraphy. Arabic motifs are predominant because of the influence of Islam where all works of art must be created for the glory of God. For example, the word at the center of the tile means "Allah."

right to left. Many of the letters are flowing and circular and look very attractive.

The Persian language was very important in the past. The first classics of literature were recorded in the 10th and 11th centuries. In the 17th century, the Persian language flourished well beyond Persian borders. This was due largely to the efforts of Shah Abbas. Under him, the Persian empire grew in political importance and in geographic dimensions. We must remember that Persia was a world power and a conquering empire. The diplomatic language for the entire Middle East and the Arab world, in general, was Persian. It became the language of culture, spoken at the court of the Turkish sultan in Istanbul as well as in Cairo, Baghdad and in India.

With the fall of the empire came a decline in the use of the Persian language. But even today, New Persian is understood as far as central Asia and India, in places like Kabul and Herat, among the Tadchiks of Afghanistan and Turkistan, and among the Hesares of central Afghanistan. Related literary languages are the Kurdish and Baluchi dialects.

Arabic calligraphy on a brass sign. It is interesting to note that although the Iranians had adopted the Arabic script for writing, the Iranian language of Farsi is totally different from Arabic and has its roots in ancient Persia.

Demonstrators hold copies of the daily Islamic newspaper, *Jomhouri Islami,* just after the revolution. The headlines read, "The Trial of the hostages is now definite." This refers to the hostages taken from the U.S. Embassy in 1979.

FARSI

Farsi is the national and official language..It is spoken as the first language by about 66% of the population. In addition, there are Turkic-speaking Azerbaijanis. Their language is called Aseri and belongs to the Turkish language group. There are other splinter groups with their own languages and dialects, such as the Kurds, Arabs, Turkomans and Baluchis which make up the remainder of the population.

In the time of Reza Shah, the father of the last Shah, there was a movement to purify the Persian language. This partly succeeded by reviving lost expressions and forgotten vocabulary. New vocabulary for

One of the common features of Iranian life is the scribe. Sitting at a bazaar or street corner in his makeshift office, he will do the reading and writing of a letter for a fee.

modern technology is largely the result of invention. English, French and Russian expressions have been adapted for use into the Farsi language.

BODY LANGUAGE

Iranians are more expressive than most people from the West. They use their hands and arms in excitement and exasperation. They hold out their arms towards a person when they want to be friendly. Their faces show anger, joy, surprise and pain very readily. Many of these symbolic gestures are influenced by social conventions and religion.

There are several Iranian body and hand gestures that differ from those in other Western countries. For example, a man may use his index finger, turning his hand up and waving to himself. This gesture, in most Western countries, means "come here." In Iran, such a gesture towards a woman is an invitation to come closer, but for suggestive reasons.

Among the signals of aggression, the simplest yet most offensive one is the "thumbs up" sign. In the United States it may mean that things are okay, that a job was well done, that something unusual has been achieved, or simply say, " Good luck." In Iran, the same signal will get you into real trouble.

On the other hand, Iranians are much more formal in many ways than people are in the United States. One of the barriers lies in gender or sex differences, another is in the importance of status. One of the major rules is that men and women must not touch each other.

ARTS

IRANIAN ART AND ARCHITECTURE have always been decorative. Through the use of symbols rather than pictures, Iran has developed its own unique style. Persian literature, especially poetry, is amazingly rich and varied. The novel appeared only in recent times as a result of European influences. Carpet and rug weaving has reached almost incredible perfection, making the name of Persia synonymous with exquisite carpets.

LANDSCAPE GARDENING

The art of landscape gardening probably had its origins in Persia. Cyrus the Great built the oldest known garden in the world. It was a carefully planned garden with a pavilion and pools and canals providing a pleasing background for beautiful trees and shrubs. Two of the most important trees that were used by early Persian gardeners were the plane and the cypress. The most popular plant was the rose, in all its glorious shapes and colors, and the jasmine which gave the gardens a lovely sweet smell. Fruit trees and vines, the most popular being grapes, peaches, figs, dates, pears and pomegranates, enhanced the appearance of the garden.

Opposite: **Unlike some other Islamic countries which frown on the representation of living things, Iranians depict human forms freely, such as on this magnificent carpet.**

Below: **One of Iran's artistic achievements is painting miniatures on paper, ceramics and even on camel bone. The pastoral scene depicted here on camel bone is a recurring theme in many paintings.**

The Koran's vision of paradise is an ideal garden with abundant fruit , rippling water, scented flowers, plenty of shady trees and young, beautiful attendants. Much of early Persian literature was filled with the visions of a paradise garden with nightingales, pavilions, fruits and flowers.

If Iran is said to be the land of poets, then Shiraz is the city of poets. This is the tomb of the famous poet Shams-ed-Hafiz. *Hafiz* means "one who remembers" and it is said that Hafiz knew the entire Koran by heart.

LITERATURE

Poetry is perhaps the most important aspect of Iranian literature. Skillful poets were famous and respected. Iranian literature reached its peak between the 10th and 16th centuries. Many significant works of philosophy, mathematics, astronomy, medicine and poetry were created although it was a period of wars and internal disorders.

Three great Iranian poets were Ferdowsi, Hafiz and Omar Khayyam. Ferdowsi wrote the *Shah-nama* (Book of Kings) about the lives of legendary kings and heroes as well as actual historical figures. Many of the copies that were made of this epic poem were illustrated with miniatures by well-known artists. Even today Iranians recite long passages of the poem.

Hafiz is, perhaps, the most popular poet in Iran. He wrote nearly 700 poems, most of which deal with religious themes. His tomb in Shiraz is now a place of pilgrimage for many Iranians who visit his tomb to seek inspiration and guidance for themselves. They open a copy of his book at random and the first line of verse that catches the reader's eye is regarded as a special message of guidance for the future.

However, the most famous Iranian poet is Omar Khayyam whose poem the *Rubáiyát* has been translated into other languages and is widely read in the Western world. Omar Khayyam was also a respected mathematician and astronomer. The local sultan or Moslem ruler was so impressed that he employed Omar to reform the calendar. This Omar did with great accuracy.

THE RUBÁIYÁT OF OMAR KHAYYAM

Ah, make the most of what we yet may spend,
Before we too into the Dust Descend;
Dust into Dust, and under Dust, to lie,
Sans Wine, Sans Song, Sans Singer and—Sans End!

Alike for those who for TODAY prepare,
And those that after some TOMORROW stare,
A Muezzin from the Tower of Darkness cries,
"Fools! your Reward is neither Here nor There."

Ah, fill the cup: what boots it to repeat
How Time is slipping underneath our Feet;
Unborn TOMORROW and dead YESTERDAY,
Why fret about them if TODAY be sweet!

The Moving Finger writes; and, having writ,
Moves on; nor all the Piety nor Wit
Shall lure it back to cancel half a Line,
Nor all thy Tears wash out a Word of it.

—Excerpts from the Rubáiyát of Omar Khayyam
(Translated from the Persian by Edward Fitzgerald)

A gateway in Persepolis portrays one of its great kings, Darius the Great, beside the mythical griffin, or winged lion.

ARCHITECTURE

The Greek historian, Herodotus, wrote in much detail about early Iranian architecture. He gave the world fascinating descriptions of early cities and their buildings. Most of these structures were made of brick. They often consisted of fire temples with fire altars reflecting the early religious beliefs. There were also descriptions of early palaces with fortresses.

Although in ruins today, Persepolis is an outstanding example of Persian architecture. The building of the ancient capital was begun by Darius in 520 B.C. and continued for nearly a century by other rulers. The city contained audience halls, gateways and other buildings. Artisans were brought from all over the empire to use their expertise in building this magnificent capital. Before the coming of Islam, stone was favored as a building material. Later, oven-baked or sun-dried bricks were used.

Abstract decoration is a major feature of Iranian architecture especially after the Moslem period. Bricks were laid in a decorative manner, sometimes in high relief, other times they were sunken. The effect was an amazingly intricate geometric pattern. Glazed colored tilework was also used to enhance the decorative brickwork.

A dome in Isfahan with traditional blue tiles. Domes, minarets and arched windows and doorways reflect the historic and religious significance of architecture in Iran.

MOSQUES

With the Arab invasion of Iran came a Moslem influence on Iranian architecture. Islamic influence was strongest between A.D. 641 and 1000. The need for a house of worship was obvious and this gave birth to the mosque.

The mosque was essentially a large open structure with arcades and a covered sanctuary within which was a "prayer niche" directing worshipers to face Mecca when they prayed. The mosque also needed a minaret from which the faithful were called to prayer.

The dome was the most important feature of Moslem architecture. It was built over the principal chamber of the mosque. Because of its awe-inspiring shape, the domes took on a symbolic religious significance. Thus, as the years went by, the domes became larger in diameter and rose higher and higher into the air. Many of the domes were covered in special blue tiles that sparkled in the sun for all travelers to see. Iranian architects also designed methods of erecting domes and vaults without using any supporting columns.

Although the mosques are splendid examples of Moslem architecture, Iranian architects also built beautiful palaces, religious schools called *madrasehs*, shrines, tombs, bridges and baths.

Students learning to paint miniatures in class.

PAINTING AND POTTERY

There are three main characteristics in traditional Iranian painting. They are highly stylized, often using abstractions, colorful and rather idealistic.

Early Persian painting was mostly confined to books. During the Safavid period, the illustrated book became a work of art with myths and legends as favorite subjects for miniature painters. Many carpet weavers often used individual design or figures in a miniature painting which they enlarged on their carpets. Traditional Iranian painting tended to portray an enchanted world where everything was perfect.

Since 1979, the trend in painting has been to move away from the ideal to more realistic representations. Early paintings depicted kings and their activities, but the modern trend is to portray ordinary people and everyday life. Modern painters express a sense of joy or sorrow using their imagination in a wider sense.

In Iran, the potter's art has existed since 6000 B.C. Several distinctive examples of ancient pottery have been found in Khorasan. These are mainly flat bowls with colorless glaze over brightly colored designs. The Islamic period in Iranian history produced exquisite pottery equal in quality to any other country of that time.

Archeologists have also uncovered numerous artifacts that are mainly stone carvings of animals and human heads. There are also small animal figures in bronze and other precious metals.

Exquisite tile work in a mosque. Iranian art is famous for its imaginative work in recreating flowers, plants and animals.

CALLIGRAPHY

Calligraphy, or the special art of writing, is held in great esteem in the Islamic world. Moslems believe that it was God who taught man to write, so to copy out parts or the whole of the Koran is a wonderful religious achievement. As God's messages were in Arabic, the script of this language became sacred. Many calligraphers enjoyed much prestige because of the association with the holy book of Islam.

THE MOST EXPENSIVE CARPET IN HISTORY

Chosroes II was a Sasanid ruler who lived in A.D. 600. He was a great lover of the arts. He commissioned an exquisite carpet for his palace at Clesiphon which was then the capital of Persia. The design was astonishing in its realism. It consisted of an enormous garden with flowerbeds, trees and even stones. Gold and silver threads represented streams; precious stones and silk created an illusion of springtime. Whatever the season, when the king entered the room, he would see the colors of spring. Unfortunately, the most expensive carpet in history did not last for long. Arab invaders who overthrew the Sasanid dynasty decided to cut it up into manageable pieces so that they could carry them away as part of the booty of war.

THE ART OF CARPET WEAVING

Iranian or Persian carpets are famous all over the world. They are not designed just to be useful and pleasant, but also as works of art.

The general Islamic emphasis on geometry and straight lines is not common in Iranian carpets. Curling flowers and tendrils with animals and men are more common. (Although other Moslem countries imposed a ban on any representation of living things, Iran's Shiite Moslems rejected this ban and used human figures quite frequently.) Traditional carpets of the 16th and 17th centuries were adorned with twittering birds and sweet smelling-flowers reflecting a beautiful garden to remind them of Paradise— a Persian word associated with the idea of a beautiful garden.

The color or the dye used in rug-making is all important. Most dyes are made from plants or insects. Here is a list of colors and their meanings:
- white—mourning, death, grief
- black—destruction
- orange—devotion and piety
- red—happiness and wealth
- brown—fertility

A carpet merchant in the bazaar. Persian carpets are said to be the best in the world. They are exported to many countries and bring very high prices.

A group of musicians play at a village festival.

IRANIAN MUSIC

Traditionally, musicians in Iran have never enjoyed a high social position. Music was played on special occasion like weddings and circumcision ceremonies. Stringed instruments often accompanied the singers. Vocal music with improvisation is a very important aspect of traditional Iranian music. The songs are often mournful. At weddings, guests are often entertained by vulgar songs.

Folk music is found in the villages where peasants take part in feasting and merrymaking to celebrate a festival or a special family occasion. Male dancers entertain, sometimes dressed as females.

A special type of music is heard in the House of Strength or Zur Khaneh.

Drums provide vigorous background to the gymnastics that are performed and verses are recited to stirring music.

Classical music in Iran never enjoyed the patronage of royal rulers as it did in other countries. It is mainly grave and mournful with religious themes or solos based on tragic stories from Iran's past.

One of the most important features of Iranian music is religious recitation. The ability to recite the whole of the Koran is greatly admired. Children from young are taught to recite verses from the Koran and when they get older they are encouraged to take part in Koran reading performances or competitions. These are often held in the fasting month of Ramadan.

A wide range of musical instruments still exists in Iran today. Some of the more popular ones are the sitar, the *santur*, the *kamenchay*, the *zarb* and the *nay*. The sitar is a lute, the *kamanchy* a spike-fiddle, the *zarb* a goblet-shaped drum, and the *nay* a flute. The *santur*, a 72-string musical instrument, is very popular in Iran even today. Most of these musical instruments are also found in the northern Indian subcontinent.

A group of dancers from a nomadic tribe, dressed in all their splendid finery, perform for their chieftain's wedding.

LEISURE

THE CONCEPT OF LEISURE in the Western sense of the word cannot be strictly applied to Iran. Historical heritage, religious beliefs and geographical setting have helped to create a diverse and varied way of life which is uniquely Iranian.

Opposite: **Two old men enjoy the fresh breezes and while their time away recalling old times and friends by the Caspian Sea.**

ENTERTAINING AT HOME

Iranians are one of the world's most hospitable people. They open their homes to strangers and provide them with as much as they can afford. The home is the center of all pleasurable activities with women cooking wonderful Iranian food for others to enjoy. The best Iranian cooking is not found in restaurants but in the home.

A meal is often a leisure activity in itself. Friends linger over a meal discussing daily affairs. Sometimes guests may be invited to a game of chess. (Iranians believe that the ancient game of chess began in Iran. However, Indians too have a similar claim!)

Above: **Family gatherings are great fun for both adults and children. It is a time to catch up on the latest gossip, to exchange news and, later in the evening, to feast.**

Since 1979, alcohol has been banned in Iran because Islam prohibits the drinking of any liquor. Instead tea-drinking is very popular, with the samovar always on the boil.

Iranians do not read as much as their Western counterparts. This is partly due to the lack of libraries, especially in rural areas. However, they love listening to the radio and watching television. All programs, though, are carefully censored by the government. This is to prevent the influence of non-Islamic values or the depiction of violence and premarital sex.

Iranians are great sports fans and support their country during international competitions in sports ranging from soccer to wrestling.

SPORTS

Modern competitive sports were almost non-existent in Iran until World War I. When Christian missionaries visited the Middle East, they brought with them Western-style sports. People began to take an interest in athletics, tennis, basketball and swimming. Soldiers of the two wars further encouraged these sports. Soccer became extremely popular and nowadays it is common to see children kicking a ball along the tree-lined streets of Iran.

Tennis and squash are also popular with Iranians. Squash is a more recent game favored by urban Iranians who work out after a hard day's work in the office. Many air-conditioned courts have been built to cater to this growing demand. In schools, gymnastics is actively encouraged and is growing in popularity. Along the coastal regions, sailing is taken up by more affluent Iranians.

However, Iranians do continue to play traditional sports whenever appropriate. In the rural areas, for example, camel and horseracing are some leisure activities that are pursued even today. Falconry and hunting are not as common as they once were, but some Iranians still train eagles or hawks for the sport of falconry.

Wrestling Iranian-style and polo are both ancient sports that are still popular today. Soccer and wrestling are popular spectator sports while polo is a game for the wealthier Iranians.

THE SPORT OF SHAHS

Iran and China both developed the sport of falconry more than 3,000 years ago. This art of training falcons, hawks or eagles requires much patience and skill as these birds of prey have to be tamed to obey the trainer. Straps around the feet restrain the bird and a hood covers its eyes to keep it calm. Bells are hung round the bird's neck or leg for tracking its location. When the falconer sights a possible prey, he releases the bird, which flies in pursuit.

In ancient Persia, falconry was the sport of the Shahs and nobility. The wide expanse of the deserts were ideal for this sport. In modern times, falconry is not so popular as guns have replaced the birds and shooting has developed into a popular sport.

HORSE-BALL

The game of polo began over 2,000 years ago. It was played by teams of four men on each side hitting a ball with sticks from horseback. The players had to be skillful horsemen as the game was usually played at full gallop. The Shahs of Iran loved to watch the game seated in the comforts of a pavilion. In fact, the city of Isfahan is said to have been planned around the royal polo ground. Even today, ancient stone goal posts, eight yards apart, still stand on the site of the polo square. The rule that the ball must be struck at full gallop was introduced in Iran.

Polo eventually found its way to northern India where British army officers stationed during the period of British rule in India gave it the name "polo" by which name it is presently known. Today, the game of "horse-ball" is enjoyed by many all over the world.

LEISURE ACTIVITIES IN THE RURAL AREAS

Village people make their own entertainment. Often their leisure activities are an extension of their work, so that joy in daily activities becomes as much a leisure activity as well as working for a living.

Few village children read books or play with toys. Most children help with chores around the house or on the farms. In the evenings, children may

amuse themselves with traditional games handed down from their forefathers or indulge in kicking a ball around.

Sometimes a traveling group of actors may go around the villages reciting poetry or performing plays about Iran's past. Stories are told of the battles won and lost, of heroes in Iran's glorious history. Once upon a time the snake charmer performed his tricks to the music of a flute-like instrument, but this is seldom seen in modern Iran. Periodically, races are held at villages to celebrate a festival or a special occasion. This could be simple athletics, or camel and horseracing.

Nomadic tribes have integrated their leisure activities into their way of life. When the day's work is completed, the family may weave rugs or simply chat over a strong glass of tea. Shepherds of goats and sheep may indulge in hunting, but this is also becoming rarer as many animals have been hunted out of existence.

Most villages have a mosque. Many Iranians will gather there on Fridays for prayers. They socialize after their prayers. Sometimes people may go to a bathhouse. These are built underground at the source of a hot water spring. The bathhouses are purely for bathing and relaxing.

As clans are more common in rural areas, these village children spend much of their time playing with their cousins and have no lack of friends.

THE HOUSE OF STRENGTH

The House of Strength or Zur Khaneh, as it is known in Iran, is supposed to have originated because of the Arab invasion of Persia. It began as a secret society whose young male members swore to drive out the foreigners. Members have vigorous training, doing strenuous exercises to the accompaniment of drumbeats and the chanting of verses from an ancient text. They wield heavy clubs, juggling them around with great speed and dexterity.

   Each House of Strength has one large room containing a wrestling pit. There is a platform for the drummer and a space for spectators. The men wear colorful knee-length trousers. The end of each session is signified by a wrestling match in both traditional and modern European styles.

In the villages and among nomadic tribes, leisure hours are spent productively weaving carpets, clothes and, like this Kurdish girl, spinning wool.

LEISURE ACTIVITIES IN THE CITIES

The intense heat in the summertime compels most Iranians to carry out their leisure activities mostly in the cool of the evenings or sometimes in the mornings.

Women seldom take part in leisure activities outside the home as household chores take up much of their time. However, a visit to the bazaar to haggle over the price of goods or to the mosque to talk with people is a welcome break from the routine of everyday life. As family life is fairly relaxed, women enjoy passing their time entertaining family and friends. Sometimes the women spend the evenings in some form of craft work such as rug weaving. Listening to music on the radio is also a popular pastime.

Iranian men love to spend their leisure time simply relaxing and watching the world go by. This is best done in the numerous teahouses that were once coffee houses called *kafekhanna*. While talking to friends, Iranian men may indulge in one of the most relaxing pastimes—smoking the hubble-bubble pipe or hookah. The purpose of the hubble-bubble is to cool the smoke by passing it through water before it is inhaled.

The entrance to a bazaar. For city folks, shopping for the home is a leisure activity. These days, it is becoming more common to have the shopping done in new shopping centers as well as in bazaars.

All Iranians love picnics. The climate is mostly dry and the outdoors can be enjoyed at most times of the year. A rug, some finger food, tea and soft drinks are all that is needed for a picnic to remind them of Paradise.

Outdoors or indoors, Iranians love to play chess. The game began in India about 400 B.C. but the Iranians took up the game soon after. They used the word "*shah*" for the chess piece called "the king" and from this comes the word "chess." The word checkmate also comes from an ancient Iranian word "*shahmat*" meaning "the king is helpless."

In recent times, the cinema has provided entertainment for the populace. Once upon a time, Western films were popular, but most of them are now banned. The majority of the films are brought in from India, Turkey and sometimes Egypt. Censorship of films is strict.

A samovar is a metal urn, usually made of copper.

A GLASS OF TEA

Iranians were once great coffee drinkers but tea has long replaced coffee as a national drink. As alcohol is prohibited (since 1979, by law) tea and soft drinks are popular both at home and at picnics or cafes. Relaxing over a glass of tea is Iran's favorite pastime. A samovar, or urn, is always on the boil in the homes, teahouses, government offices and bazaars. Most picnickers will lug a samovar with them even on a hot day. The tea not only helps to quench their thirst, but helps them feel relaxed.

Tea in Iran is seldom served in cups. It is usually served in small glasses with plenty of sugar. The tea drinker places lumps of sugar on the tongue and sips the tea drawing great pleasure from both the smell and taste of the strong tea.

The custom of drinking tea in Iran is a relatively recent event. It was introduced probably from Russia in the 19th century. Before this, most Iranians were coffee drinkers like other Moslems in the Middle East.

FESTIVALS

RELIGIOUS FESTIVALS AND HOLIDAYS play a major part in the traditional life of an Iranian family. The depth of faith demanded by Islam is evident in the number of holidays which are based on religion. Most holy days commemorate some aspect of the life and teaching of the founder, Mohammed. However, soon after Islam was founded, the Iranians showed their independence by founding a different version of the religion which they called Shia. *Shia* means party, and the Shiites belong to the party of Ali ibn Abi Talib, the son-in-law of Mohammed and his chosen successor. Ali had two sons, Hussein and Hassan who were to assume leadership after he died. As a result of their untimely deaths, Iranian Moslems tend to commemorate some religious events with mourning, remembering the suffering of the founders and leaders of this particular branch of Islam.

Opposite: **An Iranian woman prays at home during Ramadan, the holy month of fasting.**

Below: **All dressed up for a village festival in Mazandaran in northern Iran.**

However, not all Iranian celebrations are religious. The New Year Festival of Now Ruz ("no-ROOS"), for example, dates back to pre-Islamic days, to the time of Zoroastrianism when fire worshiping was important. It is the most important Iranian festival. Then there are holidays to celebrate important political events in Iran's history since the fall of the Shah. These occasions are usually celebrated with as much pomp and ceremony as the Shiite religion will allow.

Every year, Moslems all over the world sacrifice a lamb to recall Abraham's faith in and submission to God.

MOHAMMED AND ABRAHAM

The Prophet's birthday is usually celebrated in the mosque rather than in the home. Special prayers are held and, sometimes, a religious leader may take the opportunity to remind all worshipers of their Islamic beliefs and duties. In the home, stories are told about Mohammed's life, his parents and his birth. The day is usually spent quietly.

The death of Mohammed is not commemorated the way Christians remember Christ's crucifixion on the cross. Instead they remember the ascension of Mohammed called *Leilat al Meiraj*. Sometimes this Moslem festival is commemorated by women visiting graves, cleaning the area around, if necessary, and placing flowers.

Another somber celebration is that of Eid al-Adha or the feast of the sacrifice. This celebration remembers Abraham's willingness to sacrifice his son in obedience to God's command. Abraham is a patriarch well known both to Christians and Moslems as the Old Testament is common to both religions. God wanted to test Abraham's faith, so he asked him to sacrifice his son Ishmael to God at Mina, near Mecca.

The Moslem version tells of how, filled with anguish and love for his son, Abraham was about to offer his son for sacrifice when a voice called out to him to stop. An angel appeared before Abraham with a lamb and offered it in place of his son. Thankfully, Abraham took the animal. Thus, on this day, Moslems sacrifice an animal, usually a lamb or a young goat, to mark this event. As all Moslems regard the taking of life as sacred, prayers must be said while the animal is killed in a prescribed way.

RAMADAN AND EID AL–FITR

Ramadan is the most sacred month in the Moslem lunar calendar. During the whole of this month, every day at the first streak of dawn, all Moslems must abstain from eating, drinking and smoking. They must also abstain from all pleasures of the flesh. When the last rays of the sun disappear, Moslems are allowed to eat and drink as much as they want and for as long as they like but not beyond sunrise the next day. Some Iranians are so strict about observing the fast that they will not even swallow spit when fasting. The sick and pregnant women are exempted from the observation of Ramadan.

The 21st and 22nd days of the month of Ramadan are observed by Shiites as days of mourning. This is in the memory of the martyrdom of Ali, the Prophet's son-in-law. During those two days, devout followers will go round the streets beating their breasts and wailing.

Ramadan ends with the sighting of the new moon. Usually a religious leader or an elderly person will make the announcement that the fast is over. Then begins perhaps the gayest Moslem festival called Eid al-Fitr. Iranian sweets and snacks which have been prepared well ahead, will be placed on gaily decorated tables and everyone is invited to eat as much as they want to relieve the tension of the fast.

Eid al-Fitr is a very relaxed celebration. However, the true meaning of this religious function is not forgotten. Moslems usually attend community prayers held either in a mosque or in an open space. Before attending the prayers, all devout Moslems will make sure that they have cleansed themselves thoroughly, put on clean clothes and given alms to the poor or to needy relatives. Once the religious observances are over, the rest of the day is spent in joyous rounds of feasting in the company of friends and relatives.

The mosque is where most festivals of religious significance begin. The call to prayer and to giving alms extend to celebrations of the home where people are encouraged to be charitable and to welcome all to share the food in the house.

Dancing girls take a rest during the Festivities of Now Ruz.

NOW RUZ

Now Ruz is the Iranian New Year which is celebrated on March 21—the first day of spring. All Iranians look forward to this day anticipating better times and good luck.

Preparations for Now Ruz are a busy time for Iranian women. Seeds of wheat or lentil have to be planted in a shallow saucer 15 days before the festival begins. When green shoots emerge, they herald the first day of spring.

There are also other activities to be completed. All the houses are given a thorough cleaning inside and out. Rugs are dried in the sun and the dust beaten out of them. Curtains are taken down and washed. Sometimes Now Ruz is an excuse to buy new furniture or curtains for the house.

Everyone, rich or poor, will buy new clothes for themselves and for those less fortunate. Business people will give gifts to their employees hoping this generosity will bestow upon them good luck for future business. Every household also burns candles, one for each room, to create an atmosphere of joy and celebration. A special table is set aside with a candle and a mirror in the center. The Holy Koran, a bowl of water and a floating leaf, fruits and colored items are also placed on the table.

Family members gather together to await the exact time signifying the New Year. The rotating of an egg on a mirror and the movement of the leaf on the water are special signs that Iranians view as the start of the New Year. Quite often in bigger cities and towns, a cannon is fired or a gong sounded to herald the New Year.

The New Year period is a time for socializing. Friends and relatives visit uninvited to wish others a happy New Year. Old quarrels are forgotten and forgiveness is the main theme. Children enjoy this period most of all. Some are given money or gifts. Older members of the house usually remain home in the first few days of the New Year in order to receive guests. Usually the table is set up with lots of Iranian sweets and drinks. Callers come in a continuous stream from early morning to late evening. Overeating is the norm as friends are encouraged to eat more of the specially-made delectables.

The 13th day of the New Year is considered an unlucky day. In order to keep bad luck out of the house the bowls of green shoots are thrown out of the house and most families embark on a picnic outdoors. An elaborate picnic lunch is packed and families set out by car or bus for some pleasing spot away from the home hoping to take away all the bad luck for the day.

During the observance of Muharram, devotees will inflict pain by flogging their bodies or piercing their skin with hooks.

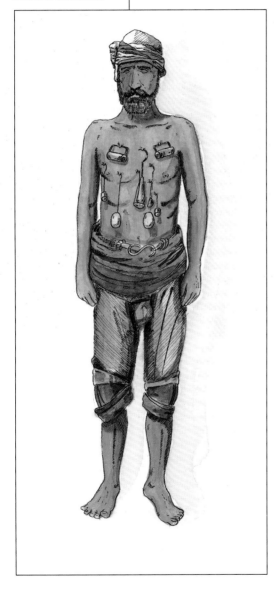

MUHARRAM

Muharram is the anniversary of the martyrdom of the prophet's grandsons Hussein and Hassan. While Moslems all over the world mourn the murder of these two men, the Shiites consider the killing of Hussein at Karbala, by an army sent by the Umayyad caliph Yazid I, a particularly dreadful crime, and so mourn his death in a very public show of sorrow lasting a whole month. Mourners join a procession through the streets giving themselves over to frenzied expressions of grief, beating themselves and sometimes even drawing blood. Sermons are also given at public places and mosques re-enforcing the teachings of Mohammed and highlighting stories about the sufferings of Hassan and Hussein.

The Shiites mark the tragedy of Karbala with passion plays called *ta'ziyeh*. These plays are usually acted out in three acts. The first act deals with the events before the battle of Karbala, the second deals with the battle itself and the last act deals with the events following the battle.

To commemorate the tragic circumstances of the martyrs' deaths, many well-to-do Iranians donate money and goods to the poor. Some hold feasts where the poor can be fed. Because it is a time of mourning no weddings or parties are held during Muharram. Some men wear black and red is forbidden.

NATIONAL HOLIDAYS

National holidays usually celebrate some major events in the recent history of Iran. On February 11, the holiday is to celebrate the fall of the Shah who was driven into exile, accused of being too Westernized. In March is Oil Nationalization Day when all Western countries who had any control of oil in Iran were also driven out and their possessions taken over by the state. Then in April, two national holidays are celebrated: Revolution Day and Islamic Republic Day. Both days bring people out into the streets in huge numbers. Most carry placards showing life-sized or even larger than life-sized pictures of their beloved leader—the Ayatollah Khomeini. In the past, Khomeini himself would appear on the balcony and everyone would cheer so loudly that often his message to the people was drowned out in a frenzy of screaming. Quite often, these public demonstrations of loyalty to their leader also reflected whatever hatred the people and their leaders may have had for countries that were enemies of the revolution. Even today, Western countries are often targets of their disapproval and this is seen in placards carrying anti-Western slogans.

When the demonstrations die down, many Iranians are happy to return home and reflect quietly on the day's activities over a glass of tea or smoke a water pipe in a cafe, gossiping with others until late in the night.

The church of St Thaddeus is one of the few places of worship and celebration for the 0.1% of Christians in Iran.

115

FOOD

Opposite: **A boy carries freshly-baked** *naan* **or bread.**

Below: **The bazaars and markets of Iran are often located along mazes of narrow lanes—providing all manners of goods and produce.**

FOOD, GLORIOUS FOOD is what Marco Polo thought when he sampled the famous melons of Iran, then known as Persia. The variety of melons grown is incredible and some of the street stalls specialize in selling only melons. But apart from melons, Iranian food is often regarded as the most refined of all Middle Eastern cuisines.

The home is the heart of Iranian cuisine. Each home has its own unique style of preparing highly imaginative dishes, the secrets of which were handed down from mother to daughter. Iranian cuisine is very old. It has developed from the early days of the first ancient Persian empire and gained sophistication down through the centuries.

External influences have, of course, affected the development of Iranian cuisine. Some areas in the south serve curries, an influence from India, while the Arab influence is more evident in the areas around the Persian Gulf. Near the borders of Turkey and Azerbaijan, Turkish influence is obvious.

117

A vegetable seller sells his produce off the back of a donkey.

PERSIAN FOOD

Iranians do not eat pork because their religion forbids it and they do not eat much beef either because the country lacks pastures that can support a sizeable herd of cattle. Lamb is the favorite meat of Iranian families and it is often slaughtered when only a few days old. In the desert, lamb is slaughtered just before a meal, then spit-roasted over an outdoor fire. In the cities, Iranians can purchase a live lamb, sheep or goat and slaughter it themselves. If it is for roasting, the lamb is usually stuffed with a mixture of rice, almonds, currants and pine nuts. Occasionally, Iranians may roast the hump of a camel if it is available. Apparently it is delicious.

One of the most popular dishes in Iran is *chelo kebab*. Tender boneless lamb is the traditional meat used for the kebab. Metal skewers are used to thread the meat together with vegetables. The meat is usually marinated in a spice-laced yogurt mixture before cooking. The kebabs are grilled over hot coals and then served on a bed of rice together with side dishes of raw onions and cucumber. Marinated chicken on a skewer is called *jujeh kebab*.

118

Around the Caspian Sea, fish is the most popular dish. Trout is popular but sturgeon is considered best and is known all over the world. Many Iranian fishermen have their own stories about the sturgeon they caught in their nets claiming that sturgeon can live to be a century old and that they each can weigh over a ton. The roe or eggs of the sturgeon is a delicacy that is too expensive for most Iranians and much of it is exported.

PERSIAN INFLUENCE ON INDIAN CUISINE

When the Moghuls invaded India and established the Moghul Empire, they brought with them not only the religion of Islam but also the much admired cuisine of Persia which they soon introduced to northern India. "Mughulai" cuisine is well known for its unique style of presentation with mountains of rice streaked with saffron and garnished with nuts, raisins and silver leaf, and meat dishes cooked in a particular style with rich smooth sauces. *Kurmah, kofta, briani* and *pilaus* are common to both Iranians and northern Indians.

Naan is a roundish flat bread that looks like oversized pancakes. They are stacked in a pile in front of bakeries and are also sold by hawkers on foot and bicycles.

RICE AND BREADS

Rice is the oldest grain in the world and is the most important item in the daily diet of most Iranians. It is relatively cheap as most of it is grown locally, mostly on the Caspian Coast. As it is the chief source of energy, it is consumed in large amounts. At a typical Iranian meal, a person's plate will be covered by a mountain of cooked rice, leaving a little space to hold small servings of vegetables, meat or fish.

Nowhere in the world (except perhaps in India) is so much time and care devoted to the preparation of rice dishes. There are two national rice dishes, *chelo* and *polo*. *Chelo* is boiled rice and when served with a special sauce it is called *chelo khoresh*. The sauce is a subtle blend of vegetables and meats, sweetened or soured by the juices of pomegranates, apples, quinces and unripe grapes. *Polo* is another Iranian national dish which is also known as *pilau* in the rest of the Middle East and northern India. It is aromatic rice cooked with several ingredients which could include any combination of vegetables, fruits, nuts, meats or duck and chicken.

The variety of unleavened bread in Iran is amazing. Bread shops are usually small with a simple griddle to cook the breads or an oven to bake them. They are of different shapes and sizes. There is the coarse bread called *sang-gak* which is made of wholemeal flour and baked over hot stones. *Naan* is an oval shaped pancake-like bread which is either baked or cooked over a bed of small stones. The "dimpled" oval breads are called *naan sangak*. The bread man usually makes delivery of the different types of bread on a specially adapted bicycle, motorcycle or van. Iranian bread is often sold by weight.

SIDE DISHES AND SOUPS

Side dishes are an essential part of the Iranian cuisine as strictly speaking Iranian dishes are not categorized into entrees and main courses. The main dishes of rice or bread are extended to include a wide range of side dishes depending on the number of people sitting down to a meal.

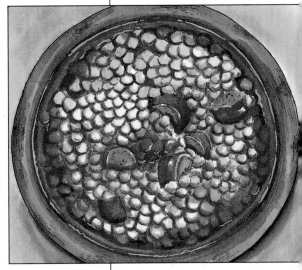

Chickpeas are normally eaten as a side dish.

Vegetable side dishes vary from region to region with eggplants and spinach very popular in most areas. Raw onions and shallots are often served with rice dishes. Stuffed vegetables called *dolmeh* are convenient finger foods which can be taken on a picnic. Eggs are a versatile side dish. They are usually beaten together with finely chopped vegetables and herbs and then made into a very thick omelette. This is cut up and served as pieces easily handled with the fingers. *Koftas* are meatballs, but these are no ordinary meatballs. They are usually finely minced mutton or lamb, highly spiced with the addition of herbs and stuffed with a mixture of fried onions, currants and chopped nuts. Often, in the center is a whole peeled, boiled egg.

Soups are very popular with all Iranians. Sometimes they are served with a meal or a worker will be satisfied with a hearty mutton soup thickened with chickpeas, called *abgoosht* ("up-GOOSHT"). Chickpeas are a side dish with both bread and rice. They are either served boiled after being soaked for several hours or pureed with oil and used as a dip for breads.

IRANIAN DRINKS AND SWEETS

After a hearty meal, Iranians indulge in a wide range of fruits available to them—pomegranates, quinces, pears, grapes, dates, apricots, peaches and, of course, the famous Iranian melons. The fruits are usually offered sliced, sometimes sweetened with rose water, or crushed and served as a colorful sherbet.

In Shiraz, a rose-flavored ice drink laced with lemon juice is called palouden. Rose essence and rose water are used in many Iranian dishes. The essence is extracted from a variety of special roses. Of course, the ever popular yogurt drink and tea is a favorite during the very hot months.

Iranians have a sweet tooth but their desserts are not as sweet as the traditional sweets of the Middle East. They are usually specially made for festive occasions and holidays. Halva, common to the Middle East, is very

YOGURT, THE PERSIAN MILK

Yogurt was part of Iranian cuisine from early days when it was referred to as "Persian milk." Nearly all yogurt is homemade and is used widely in cooking and for general consumption. It has found its way into Iranian cuisine in a variety of different guises.

The enzyme contained in yogurt is the ingredient that helps to break up meat tissues, tenderizing the meat in the process. It also helps spices to penetrate deep into the meat enhancing the flavor of the meat dish.

The most suitable yogurt is made from whole milk and is thick set. If the fat is extracted as in non-fat yogurt then the gravy is too watery. Iranian yogurt is usually rich and creamy in taste.

Yogurt is used in cold and hot soups. Sometimes it is whisked with water and mint to make a wonderfully cool drink for hot summer days. Yogurt is also used in salads—in fact in nearly everything!

Iranians claim that yogurt cures ulcers, relieves sunburn and is a supposed remedy for malaria. Young girls use yogurt as a face mask and health conscious Iranians drink it to prolong their life. No wonder Iranians consider yogurt a miracle food!

A fruit market in the bazaar. Iran is a garden of fruits with apples, tangerines, grapes, peaches and pomegranates grown for local consumption and export.

popular in Iran. It is made of flour, shortening, sugar and nuts and lasts a long time. Baklava is another sweet common to the Middle East but the Iranian variety is smaller and is less sweet. Nuts, raisins and preserved fruits are snack foods for Iranians looking for something to nibble or in between meals or over a glass of strong Iranian tea. Tea is served, watered down with a little salt and sometimes an herb to spice it up. Tea is the national drink and is drunk throughout the year.

IRAN

Abadan A3
Atrak C1
Azerbaijan A1

Bakhtaran A2
Baluchistan D3
Bandar Abbas C4

Caspian Sea B1

Dash-e-Kavir Desert C2
Dash-e-Lut Desert C3

Elburz Range B2

Fars B3

Gulf of Oman C4

Hamadan A2

IranShahr D4
Isfahan B2

Karun A3	Mashhad C1	Rafsanjan C3	Tabriz A1
Khorasan C2	Mt. Damavand B2		Tehran B2
Khuzestan A3		Safid B1	
	Persian Gulf B4	Sahand Mt. A1	Yazd B3
Lake Bakhtegan C3		Shiraz B3	
Lake Sistan D3	Qom B2	Sistan D3	Zagros Mountains B2
Lake Urmiyeh A1			

— International Boundary
▲ Mountain
● Capital
● City
✕ River
⌒ Lake

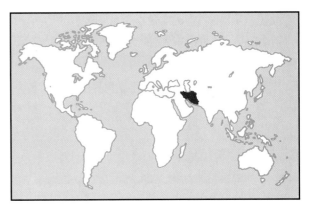

QUICK NOTES

AREA
636,296 square miles

POPULATION
52,000,000

CAPITAL
Tehran

OFFICIAL NAME
Islamic Republic of Iran

OFFICIAL LANGUAGE
Farsi or Persian

NATIONAL DISTRICTS
Bakhtaran, Bushehr, Chahar Mahal Va Bakhtiari, East Azerbaijan, Fars, Gilan, Hamadan, Hormuzgan, Ilam, Isfahan, Kerman, Khorasan, Khuzestan, Kohkil Uyeh Va Boyer Ahmad, Lorestan, Marzaki, Mazandaran, Semnan, Sistan Va Baluchistan, West Azerbaijan, Yazd, Zanjan

MAJOR RELIGION
Shiite Islam

SECTS OF ISLAM
Shiite
Sunni

HIGHEST POINT
Mount Damavand (18,386 feet)

MAJOR LAKES
Bakhtegan Lake, Jaz Murian Lake, Sistan Lake and Urmiyeh Lake

MAJOR RIVERS
Atrak, Karun, Safid

CURRENCY
100 Dinars = 1 Rial
10 Rials = 1 Toman
(US$1= 72.2 Rials)

MAIN EXPORTS
Oil, wheat, barley, rice, caviar, potatoes, cotton, citrus fruits, pistachios, corn and tea.

POLITICAL LEADERS
Reza Shah—Shah of Iran and founder of the Pahlavi dynasty (1925–1941)
Mohammed Reza Shah Pahlavi—the last Shah of Iran (1941–1979)
Ayatollah Khomeini—first *wali faqi* of the Islamic Republic of Iran (1979–1989)
Ayatollah Khamenei—current *wali faqi*
Ali Akbar Rafsanjani—current prime minister

GLOSSARY

Ayatollah   Title given to pious and learned religious men at the top of the Islamic Shiite hierarchy.

bazaar   A traditional marketplace.

qanats   Underground water tunnels.

majlis   Literally "council;" a consultative assembly of elected representatives.

muezzin   An official of the mosque, proclaiming the hour of prayer.

mullah   A Moslem teacher or scholar.

hookah   Water pipe for smoking.

Shah   A sovereign of Iran.

ulema   A religious leader in the mosque.

BIBLIOGRAPHY

Husain, A.: *A Revolution in Iran,* Rourke, Vero Beach, FL, 1991.

Lerner Publications: Department of Geography Staff, *Iran in Pictures,* Lerner, Minneapolis, MN, 1989.

Manneti, Lisa: *Iran and Iraq: Nations at War,* Franklin Watts, New York, 1986.

Miller, William M.: *Tales of Persia: A Book for Children,* Presbyterian and Reformed, Phillipsburg, NJ, 1988.

Sanders, Renfield: *Iran,* Chelsea House, New York, 1990.

INDEX